Miracles and the Concept of Impossibility

The Resurrection and the Shroud of Turin

Anthony Walsh, Ph.D.
Boise State University

With a Foreword by
Pastor Rick Flood
Compelled Church, Temperance, Michigan

Series in Philosophy of Religion
VERNON PRESS

Copyright © 2023 Vernon Press, an imprint of Vernon Art and Science Inc, on behalf of the author.

All rights reserved. No part of this publication may be reproduced, stored in a retrieval system, or transmitted in any form or by any means, electronic, mechanical, photocopying, recording, or otherwise, without the prior permission of Vernon Art and Science Inc.

www.vernonpress.com

In the Americas:
Vernon Press
1000 N West Street, Suite 1200
Wilmington, Delaware, 19801
United States

In the rest of the world:
Vernon Press
C/Sancti Espiritu 17,
Malaga, 29006
Spain

Series in Philosophy of Religion

Library of Congress Control Number: 2022950720

ISBN: 978-1-64889-618-7

Also available:

Hardback: 978-1-64889-598-2

Product and company names mentioned in this work are the trademarks of their respective owners. While every care has been taken in preparing this work, neither the authors nor Vernon Art and Science Inc. may be held responsible for any loss or damage caused or alleged to be caused directly or indirectly by the information contained in it.

Cover design by Vernon Press. Cover image by Fathromi Ramdlon from Pixabay.

Every effort has been made to trace all copyright holders, but if any have been inadvertently overlooked the publisher will be pleased to include any necessary credits in any subsequent reprint or edition.

Table of Contents

	Foreword	vii
	Acknowledgements	ix
	Preface	xi
Chapter 1	**Miracles and the Concept of Impossibility**	1
	David Hume and Miracles	1
	When the Improbable Becomes the Impossible	4
	Natural Theology	6
	Notes	10
Chapter 2	**The Miraculous Impossible Universe**	13
	The Unnatural Standard Model of Particle Physics	13
	The Big Bang	15
	Early Opposition to the Big Bang	16
	Other Miraculous Facts About the Universe	17
	The Sun	19
	Atheist Response: The Multiverse	21
	Atheist Response: Who Made God?	22
	Notes	23
Chapter 3	**The Miracle of Life**	25
	Life: Rising from Dead Matter	25
	Amino Acids to Proteins	26
	The Cell and DNA	28
	Carbon: It's Incredibly Improbable Existence	29
	Theistic Evolution	31
	The Miracle of You	32
	Notes	35

Chapter 4	**The Atonement, Hell, and Universal Salvation**	37
	The Atonement	37
	Hell	38
	John Calvin and Predestination	42
	Universalist Eschatology	43
	Why the Debate?	47
	Notes	49
Chapter 5	**The Resurrection: The Event that Changed Everything**	51
	The Bedrock of Christianity	51
	The Nature of Historical Explanation	52
	The Minimal Facts of the Resurrection	54
	The Resurrection and Miracles	55
	Evidence from the New Testament	56
	The Bible and the Archaeological Record	59
	Notes	60
Chapter 6	**Secular Attempts to Explain the Resurrection**	63
	The Stolen Body Theory	63
	The Wrong Tomb Theory	65
	The Fraud or Conspiracy Theory	66
	The Swoon Theory	66
	The Legend Theory	67
	The Hallucination Theory	69
	The Conversion Disorder and Bereavement Visions Theories	71
	Notes	73
Chapter 7	**The History of the Shroud of Turin**	75
	Introduction to the Shroud of Turin	75
	The Shroud and the Image of Edessa	76
	Is the Image of Edessa and the Shroud of Turin the Same Cloth?	79

	The Sudarium of Oviedo	80
	The Hungarian Pray Manuscript	81
	Images: Acheiropoieta and Photographs	83
	Notes	84
Chapter 8	**Scientific Testing of the Shroud of Turin**	85
	The Shroud of Turin Research Project	85
	Carbon-14 Dating of the Shroud	87
	The Mysteries of the Image	89
	Blood, Forensic Pathology, and Pollen Evidence	91
	What are we to Conclude?	93
	Notes	95
	References	97
	Index	105

Foreword

When I first met Anthony (Tony), it was following a weekend gathering in which I had led worship. I can recall him approaching me as soon as we were done; I was instantly drawn in due to his slight grin and kind posture. Our conversation started with a question, "Are you familiar with the greatest hymn ever written?" This was a difficult question to respond to as the case could be made for so many hymns. However, he followed up with the answer as fast as the question was asked, "How Great Thou Art." As we began to dialog on why this was the greatest hymn ever written, I have to admit that he was quickly winning me over with his perspective and explanation. After a great conversation, he left me with these words, "Sing it for me next weekend" with a look of jest and resolve. Tony disappeared into the crowd. I have to admit I did not sing the hymn the following weekend but I did add it to the list shortly after our conversation. The delight on his face following that gathering was amazing!

I share that story because what I have found through multiple conversations and reading Tony's material, is that this is more than just a catchy tune to him that speaks of God and creation, it is the embodiment of his awe and wonder of a great God that is full of love and compassion towards people. The lyrics of this hymn are the expression that the God of all creation is also the God of the intimate. In scripture, we find Jesus making this powerful declaration over us, Jesus replied: 'Love the Lord your God with all your heart and with all your soul and with all your mind' (Matthew 22:37). I believe that the church does an excellent job of speaking to the heart and soul side of understanding. Tony, however, is doing a great work in giving us a wonderful understanding and wisdom into the depths of who God is and who we are in relation to that revelation through the mind. The way Tony sets out to show God's existence not just through experience but also through science will be a gift to you on many levels.

One of the things that I have appreciated about this work is that while we hold some different theological positions, Tony's approach is informative as well as open minded to conversations and disagreement. For instance, we differ in our position on universalism and physical hell. My belief is that God is love as shown through the depth of the atonement provided for us, *For God so loved the world (John 3:16)*. I also believe God is just and that it would be counter to His character to overlook the sins of man. I believe salvation is offered to all people but the way of salvation is through confession: "*Believe with your heart and confess with your mouth*" *(Romans 10:9)*. I do agree that our leverage of hell and eternal damnation has gone outside the boundaries of its intent at times.

When we use hell to scare or manipulate towards salvation, we have lost our way. I also believe there is a Physical Hell; I believe those that do not turn to God will find themselves there. I don't believe this is out of an angry, abusive position from God. I truly believe that we will never fully know the heartache sin and eternal Damnation is to God until we see Him face to face. I understand the argument usage of verses stating "All Men" and the attachment to the universal argument, but I see them as opportunities for transformation more of an invitation than a declaration. It is the If/Then principle we find in scripture. "If my people, then I will". I do not see these verses as definitive proclamation cast over all people as a blanket statement of salvation. This is why I see the evangelistic call to the church as the highest importance. We must go and tell of the good news so that all may hear and know the goodness of God. It has been a joy to get to know Tony and his desire and passion for the Lord are both refreshing and encouraging in my own life.

Rick Flood

Executive Pastor

Compelled Church

Acknowledgements

I would first like to acknowledge acquisitions editor Blanca Caro for her faith in this work, and production editor Argiris Legatos for his usual great job in moving this book forward into print. I also would like to thank anonymous reviewers for their excellent criticisms and suggestions, and Grace Walsh and Rick Flood, who read all or part of the manuscript. The input from these good people has made this book better than it would otherwise have been. Of course, whatever errors that remain are mine alone. Most of all, I thank God for giving me the time, inclination, and insight to be able to complete this work. I also acknowledge the contribution of my dear wife, Grace (AKA "Grace the Face"). She takes such great care of my needs that I am able to devote far more time to writing than I would otherwise have. She makes my life heaven on earth: thank you, Gracie.

Preface

This book takes a fresh look at the miracle of the Resurrection of Jesus Christ. A miracle is a claim that something occurred that is deemed inexplicable by the normal methods of science. This being the case, most scientists and laypersons are of the opinion that miracles are highly improbable or even impossible. Scottish Enlightenment philosopher David Hume's 1748 essay *Of Miracles* is usually taken as the definitive statement about the impossibility of miracles. Hume asserted that miracles are violations of the laws of nature and of our uniform experience of them, and must thus be ruled out absolutely. If miracles are defined as impossible, it behooves us to examine what the concept of *impossibility* actually means. I am not talking about the logically impossible, but the statistically impossible.

There is a boundary of probability beyond which the improbable becomes the impossible. This has been calculated by mathematician William Dembski, who puts it at 10^{150}. This incredible figure completely exhausts all probability resources since it is the sum of all the atoms in the universe, all the seconds since the universe began, and the fastest possible time in which an event can occur (Planck time). Physicist Nima Arkani-Hamed once declared in a talk that the universe is inevitable and that it is also impossible. That sounds very much like a logical impossibility because something impossible cannot be inevitable. Yet here we are, so half of that statement is indisputably true. What about the impossible half, what could he have meant by that? He was referring to the mind-boggling improbability that a biocentric universe should exist at all. For instance, Nobel laureate physicist Sir Roger Penrose calculated the probability of the universe getting started compatible with the second law of thermodynamics (the lowest possible entropy or disorder) as 10^{10} [123]. This is many orders of magnitude beyond the probability boundary and is thus "impossible." If a miracle is defined as an impossibility, then Arkani-Hamed is right—the universe is impossible. If the universe is impossible, is it a miracle, even though is comports with our uniform experience of it?

The origin of life on this once barren rock we call home appears just as miraculously impossible. How did dead organic molecules evolve into the organic molecules of life? The optimism following the famous 1953 Miller/Urey experiment has slowly dissolved into pessimism after millions of man-hours and dollars have been spent on researching the issue. Even Urey has admitted that the more scientists look into the origin of life, the more we feel that it is too complex to have evolved. However, he does believe as an article of *faith* that life evolved and developed the metabolic and reproductive capabilities necessary to move from chemical to biological evolution. So, what is the best probability calculation for life to have come from dead matter by completely natural means? Astrophysicists Fred Hoyle and Chandra Wickramasinghe's probability calculations arrived at a statistical improbability far greater than even Penrose's for the origin of the universe. They arrived at the astounding value of one part in $(10^{20})^{2000}$, or $10^{40,000}$. To beat such an improbability is surely a miracle.

The remaining chapters examine the Resurrection event, beginning with what it means in terms of the atonement and the concept of universal salvation. After addressing those issues, I examine the historical evidence for the Resurrection and reasons why we can trust the New Testament. Historians judge the reliability of ancient documents by looking at the number of existing copies of the original text and at the time gap between the earliest existing manuscripts and the time when the original was written. A text is considered reliable to the extent that the number of existing manuscripts is large and the time gap between them and the event they portray is short. The New Testament is far closer to meeting those criteria than any other ancient document. What is more, archaeology is consistently unearthing artifacts confirming that people and places recorded in the Bible formerly considered fictitious did indeed exist.

The next two chapters address the Resurrection of Christ. First, I examine the historical evidence, that relies on the explanatory scope and power of a theory. I also address the trustworthiness of the New Testament in terms of these criteria and in terms of archaeological evidence. The second chapter considers secular explanations of the Resurrection: the wrong tomb, fraud, conspiracy, legend, "swoon," hallucination, vision, and conversion disorder hypotheses. These explanations are pitted against the Christian account in terms of their explanatory scope and power. Secular accounts purport to explain only one of the agreed-upon facts whereas the biblical explanation accounts for them all, and thus the Christian account has far greater explanatory scope and power.

The final two chapters look at the "silent witness" to the Resurrection; the Shroud of Turin. This cloth bears the image of a terribly tortured and crucified man. The first of these chapters examines the vague history of the cloth from the death of Christ to the present, and the second looks at the forensic evidence for its authenticity. For 125 years, scientists have been unable to discover how the image was imprinted on the cloth, thus I conclude that it is the "silent witness" to the Resurrection—the authentic burial cloth of Jesus Christ.

Chapter 1

Miracles and the Concept of Impossibility

David Hume and Miracles

As the Apostle Paul reminded us, the Resurrection of Jesus Christ is the foundation of the Christian faith, ushering in the promise of salvation by the Atonement for our sins by Christ's cruel death on the cross. The resurrection of a man from the dead is a miracle and the miraculous lies beyond the horizon of normal human experience. Miracles excite awe and wonder because they are events beyond the reach of natural causes, and are thus inexplicable by the language of science as normally conceived. The word *miracle* comes from the Latin word *mirari*, "to wonder." Miracles as rare events that reveal the divine at the human level of understanding. There is an abundance of historical evidence for this event, but my primary emphasis is on science because nature itself attests to no end of miracles if we define them as statistically impossible. A piece of compelling evidence for the Resurrection is the Shroud of Turin. The shroud is a large cloth containing a ghostly image of a crucified man which has defied all efforts to determine how the image got on the cloth by natural methods for 125 years. If science can easily explain how all images are formed except this one, our minds ascend to the miraculous. Because miracles are inexplicable by science, most philosophers and scientists are of the opinion that they are impossible. Denial of miracles is rooted in materialism/ naturalism, a philosophy that denies the reality of anything outside the realm of nature and the material.

Scottish Enlightenment philosopher, David Hume has been the mainstay for centuries of those who disavow the possibility of miracles. Hume's strong polemic against miracles is almost always included in anthologies dealing with the matter as if his work both began and ended the discussion of miracles even though many philosophers wrote on the subject before Hume, and many more have written after him. Hume wrote in his 1748 essay *Of Miracles*: "A miracle is a violation of the laws of nature; and as a firm and unalterable experience has established these laws, the proof against a miracle, from the very nature of the fact, is as entire as any argument from experience can possibly be imagined."[1] Hume is saying that miracles violate the laws of nature and our uniform experience of those laws and thus they must be ruled out *a priori*. This is an epistemological rather than an ontological argument. That is, it says the regularities of human experience rule out miracles without explicitly claiming they are not real.

Hume maintains that the proof against miracles is derived from the same evidence that proves the laws of nature and thus the proof against miracles is as absolute as any argument made from the regularities of experience can possibly be. For Hume, natural laws are the ultimate and only determinant of everything that happens in the universe since they are fixed and unchanging. In another place, he hints that there might be proof for miracles but that evidence must be superior to evidence against them. He concludes, however, that this would only be possible if the falsehood of the evidence (regarding the laws of nature) would be more miraculous than the event claimed as a miracle. So, the only evidence for the truth of a miracle would be the falsification of the laws of nature, and that he says would be more miraculous than the evidence of the claimed miracle. The laws of nature are indeed immutable regularities that have been proved faithful time and time again, and no one of right mind would ever claim they are false.

Does this then prove Hume to be correct? No, it does not, for as William Lane Craig says in his defense of miracles: "an event cannot be ruled out simply because it does not accord with the regular pattern of events."[2] Craig wants us to abandon the centuries-old concept of miracles as "violations" of nature: "The proper course would be to abandon the incoherent notion of a miracle as a 'violation of a law of nature' in favor of 'an event which is naturally impossible.'"[3] In other words, miracles lie "outside the productive capacity of natural causes,"[4] and if an "event is naturally impossible... it requires a supernatural cause."[5] Craig is saying that the laws of nature faithfully describe what will happen in any particular event in the universe assuming that there are no intervening supernatural factors. This view is echoed by Mackie: "The laws of nature ... describe the ways in which the world—including, of course, human beings—works when left to itself, when not interfered with. A miracle occurs when the world is not left to itself, when something distinct from the natural order as a whole intrudes into it."[6] Plantinga concurs, arguing that the laws of nature only "describe how things go when the universe is causally closed, subject to no outside causal influence. They don't purport to tell us how things always go; they tell us, instead, how things go when no agency outside the universe acts in it."[7]

What those who deny miracles ignore is that God is not subject to natural laws. God created those laws and thus cannot be held hostage to them, nor can He be accused of violating them. God gave us the laws of nature and it is His prerogative to intervene in the regularities of the natural world, and He does. Surely, it is mere child's play for a Being who created the universe to raise the dead. If you believe in God, you should have no trouble believing in miracles because the "problem" of miracles is really a matter of whether one believes in God or not. A miracle is God *intervening* in His laws of nature; not "violating" them. Another way of putting it is that a miracle is a rare and temporary suspension of the regularities of nature's laws that reveal God's purpose, presence, and power. It is still true that nothing *natural* can contravene the laws of nature, but God is *super*natural and can do as he pleases. As Jesus said: "What is impossible for mortals is possible for God" (Luke 18:27). These are not God-of-the-gaps arguments because they do not invoke God to explain *natural* events for which science has no good explanation at present. They are arguments that invoke God in the explanation of events outside of science; that is *super*natural events. God can operate beyond the capacities of the laws of nature which He ordained.

Why do we hear of so few miracles today (I won't get into the issue of the many claims of miracle cures that medical science cannot explain because they have no bearing on the topics of this book) when we read of so many in close temporal proximity in the both the Old and New Testaments? The first reason is that God must be hidden to a certain extent lest knowledge of His existence is forced on us. Philosophers and theologians have long argued that God must be at an intellectual distance (they call this *epistemic distance*) from us so that we can come to Him freely and not through coercion. Numerous awe-inspiring miracles would compel belief in everyone, and that is not what God wants. The force and inspiration of miracles reside in their rarity and that force and inspiration would be lost with constant repetition. Like the laws of nature, frequent miracles would be seen as regularities, and the distinction between the natural and the supernatural would be blurred. If this were the case, the laws of nature would come to be viewed as imprecise and untrustworthy, thus stifling scientific progress.

Second, miracles are rare events that God only performs for sufficiently grave reasons. Biblical miracles had the specific function of authenticating both God's message and His messengers at a particular historical juncture. The miracles of the Old Testament authenticated Moses and the other prophets as God's earthly voices, and the miracles of the New Testament authenticated Jesus Christ and His Gospel message of salvation. As Jesus said in revealing the purpose of His Miracles: "If I am not doing the works of my Father, then do not believe me" (John 10:37). And Mark 16: 20 notes "And they went forth, and preached everywhere, the Lord working with them, and *confirming the word by the signs* that followed" (emphasis added). When the revelation was completed and Christianity firmly established there was no further need for miracles of the kind described in the Bible.

When the Improbable Becomes the Impossible

Scientific evaluations of phenomena often involve calculating probabilities because we cannot always say that given X, Y *will* occur. This is less true in physics and chemistry than in biology, and definitely less true than in the social sciences such as psychology or sociology. What scientists usually say is that given X, Y has a certain *probability* of occurring. When scientists make observations, they are like jury members in a criminal trial instructed not to convict the offender unless convinced that he or she is guilty beyond a reasonable doubt. The common law judicial system assumes innocence until the facts indicate otherwise. Scientists also presume "innocence"—that X does *not* cause Y. This is called the null hypothesis, which they will not reject unless probability calculations tell them that they can do so "beyond a reasonable doubt."

Naturalists think of everything in the universe, including life, as the result of atoms bumping into each other in the night in a completely random way. Statistics is the method by which science deals with randomness by asking how probable is event X to come about by chance. It assigns some level of confidence by which we can say event X is or is not the result of chance. What level of confidence constitutes beyond a reasonable doubt? Jury members must weigh the pros and cons of the evidence presented before making a decision. A great deal of subjective interpretation and bias goes into the jurors' votes. They have no hard and fast objective criteria for arriving at a decision to reject or accept the assumption of innocence beyond the imprecise "reasonable doubt" rule, and they can easily reach an incorrect decision. However, scientists have very precise mathematical criteria guiding their decision to accept or reject chance. A liberal probability value would be a 0.01 confidence level, meaning that the research hypothesis that X *does* cause Y could be wrong by chance 1 out of every 100 times similar observations are made and measured. If a probability is greater than 0.01 the null hypothesis (the result is pure chance) is retained; if equal to or less than 0.01, it is rejected. A more conservative one is 0.001, or one chance in a thousand that one's results are attributable to chance. Rare events obviously happen; we just have to ask how likely or unlikely they are to happen using statistics.

Hume and other like-minded folks say that miracles are not just improbable, they are simply impossible. But if miracles are defined as events deemed beyond the realm of possibility, then there are a number of events we know have occurred that are beyond the statistically possible from a purely naturalistic perspective. If that is the case, then these events would have to be considered miracles because they exceed the boundary of probability, and only God can do that. So, what is the point at which the merely improbable becomes impossible; not just beyond a reasonable doubt, but beyond all *possible* doubt?

I'm not talking of logical impossibilities such as throwing a 13 with a standard pair of six-sided dice or asking if God can make a rock so heavy that He can't lift it. Rather, I'm talking about physical events that we typically think of as natural rather than miraculous. Scientists have made undisputed calculations regarding the origin of the universe and the origin of life and find that the probability of their existence way beyond the probability boundary; that is, just like Hume's miracles, they are "impossible," but the existence of the universe and life are not matters of debate. If our existence is deemed statistically impossible but nevertheless is an obvious fact, why can we not accept less spectacular biblical miracles, also deemed impossible, as facts?

Mathematician William Dembski computed the absolute limit of the probability of natural events occurring using three solid estimates from astrophysics. The first is the estimated number of atoms in the known universe (10^{80}). The second is Planck time (10^{-45}), and the third is the number of seconds since the beginning of time (10^{25}). These are real estimates based on hard data and some very complicated mathematics. Planck time sets an absolute limit on the rate at which elementary particles can transition from one state to another. From these absolute limits—all existing matter; the shortest period of time for any transition from one state to another, and the total time available in which everything in the universe has happened, Dembski concludes: "If we now assume that any specification of an event within the known physical universe requires at least one elementary particle to specify it and that such specifications cannot be generated any faster than the Planck time, then these cosmological constraints imply that the total number of specified events throughout cosmic history cannot exceed $10^{80} \times 10^{45} \times 10^{25} = 10^{150}$".[8] This is the probability boundary. It completely exhausts all probability resources since it includes all the atoms in the universe, all the seconds since the universe began, and the fastest possible time in which a transitional event can occur.

Exponential numbers such as 10^{150} are a lot larger than they seem to those unfamiliar with the language of exponentials. Dembski's probability boundary is 1 followed by 150 zeros. To put it in perspective, one million is 10^6, a billion is 10^9, and a trillion is 10^{12}, or 1 followed by just 12 zeros. Numbers larger than a trillion are difficult for us to wrap our minds around, but astrophysicist Hugh Ross provides us with an example we can visualize that helps us to understand the number 10^{37}, which, while immense, is vastly smaller than 10^{150}. Ross says:

> Cover the entire North American continent in dimes all the way up to the moon, a height of about 239,000 miles (in comparison, the money to pay for the U.S. federal government debt would cover one square mile less than two feet deep with dimes.). Next, pile dimes from here to the moon on a billion other continents the same size as North America.

Paint one dime red and mix it into the billions of piles of dimes. Blindfold a friend and ask him to pick out one dime. The odds that he will pick the red dime are one in 10^{37}.[9]

This brief excursion into probability was taken because I wish to show in the next two chapters that just as miracles are said to be impossible, so are many things we take for granted, such as our own existence. Numerous features of the universe are so freakishly fine-tuned for the existence of intelligent life that many physicists are beginning to come to grips with the notion that our universe is profoundly "unnatural." As physicist Nima Arkani-Hamed declared in a talk at Columbia University: "The universe is inevitable," and at the same time, "The universe is impossible."[10] How can something be both inevitable and impossible? It had to be inevitable because here we are; it is impossible because events such as the origin of the universe and the origin of life have been called "miraculous" because the probabilities they calculate for these things occurring naturally vastly exceed the probability boundary and are thus impossible without God's guiding hand. Many see these and other phenomena as expressions of divine action as more improbable than miracle accounts contained in the Bible. Yes, we are talking about natural phenomena that can be seen and measured, but as Heiko Schulz notes, everything, natural or supernatural, is done by God's will: "God can do—more precisely, God can only do—what only God can do; and miracles can be done only by God (or at least some divine power). Thus, everything done by God is and must be perceivable as a miracle."[11]

Five hundred years ago, Martin Luther saw the existence of the universe with its laws and inherent regularities to be improbable, inexplicable, extraordinary, and miraculous, and thus of great religious significance.[12] Since Luther's time, scientists have plumbed the depths of these regularities and come to understand them. They have found naturalistic explanations for them, but many, including many Nobel laureates, find them no less improbable and miraculous. We have found naturalistic explanations for these things because we live in the natural world, but the more we learn about these things the more impossible they seem. Why is there something rather than nothing when science itself tells us that our existence in the universe, or the existence of the universe itself, while within Hume's universal experience of them, is mind-bogglingly beyond the point of the statistically possible? Asking such questions takes us into the realm of natural theology.

Natural Theology

Natural theology involves observing nature and engaging science and reason to provide evidence for God's existence and Divine Providence by "reasoning to the best explanation." Using the process of abductive reasoning, it examines all the available evidence from science, history, and philosophy to arrive at the most reasonable conclusion. The phrase *theologia naturalis* (natural theology) was coined by Augustine and its classic expression is found in Thomas Aquinas' Five Ways. The Catholic Church has always championed natural theory, but it has been rejected by some Protestant denominations on the ground that it is only by God's grace that we can get to know Him. However, those who most forcefully advance natural theology in their work and on YouTube videos are Protestant apologists. Among the many such men are scientists such as mathematician John Lennox, astrophysicist Hugh Ross, physicist and Anglican priest John Polkinghorne, and theologians/philosophers such as William Craig and Keith Ward. These men affirm that we can come to know God through the light of human reason as it contemplates His beauty and creation, and it is all defiantly miraculous!

Natural theology maintains that there are two books we may use to proclaim the glory of God: the book of God's *word* (revealed scripture) and the book of God's *works* (the fingerprints of God that science has revealed to us). Natural theology thus investigates the existence of God by momentarily setting aside the revealed word (while always affirming that it must remain of primary importance) and engaging with the evidence supplied by science and philosophical reasoning to arrive at a conclusion affirming the existence of God. But as my pastor says, this is "information without transformation." Knowledge of God's existence absent a relationship with Him leads to a deistic God who is wholly "other." Yet, I believe that for atheists and agnostics who seek truth, the better initial path to God is to understand Him is "from what has been made," as in Romans 1:20: "For since the creation of the world God's invisible qualities—his eternal power and divine nature—have been clearly seen, being understood from what has been made, so that people are without excuse." Nevertheless, natural theology buttressed by archaeology and the historical record goes only so far. Certain deeply mysterious tenets of the Christian faith, such as the triune God, the virgin birth, and the dual nature of Christ, can only be grasped by faith.

To those who insist that faith in the revealed word is enough, I point to Matthew 22:37 (quoting Jesus): "You shall love the Lord your God with all your heart and with all your soul and with all your *mind.*" Many believe that a subjective experience of God is enough to justify believing in God. This kind of self-authentication can be foundational to one's faith, but many believers, troubled by the fact that human experiences are fallible, seek and welcome evidentiary support from science. Physician, geneticist, and former atheist, Francis Collins, is one who found God in his science: "I have found there is a wonderful harmony in the complementary truths of science and faith. The God of the Bible is also the God of the genome. God can be found in the cathedral or in the laboratory. By investigating God's majestic and awesome creation, science can actually be a means of worship."[13] Collins is hardly alone in this. Astrophysicist Paul Davies notes that while it may seem bizarre, science may be a better initial path to God than religion, and that "science has actually advanced to the point where what were formerly religious questions can be seriously tackled."[14] Davies' position appears to be that scientific evidence can lead people to take their faith more seriously than they otherwise may, and can lead agnostics and atheists to accept God. Even though transformative experiences have more impact, people typically do not actively seek such experiences the way they seek or encounter intellectual enlightenment.

It may be commendable to accept God on faith alone, as long as that faith is not blind faith. Real faith is based on trust, confidence, and reliance in or on, a person or thing based on evidence and experience; blind faith is belief without understanding, perception, or discrimination. The Christian can be quite comfortable believing that God has created the universe, even if he cannot make any cogent arguments for that conclusion. God does not want blind faith. He wants us to wrestle with Him like Jacob (Genesis 32:22-32); to struggle from doubt to a reasoned faith and hope. He wants the lost lamb, the prodigal son, and the doubting Thomas. We can only be able to bring them into the fold with reasoned and knowledgeable arguments from science, philosophy, and history. Doubt comes to all of us at times. There is nothing unbiblical about asking for extra-biblical evidence for our faith, nor is it an indictment of the asker's faith. After all, did not the apostle Thomas ask for evidence, and did not Jesus gladly provide it?

The fruitfulness of engaging natural theology is provided by a study of the reasons why former atheists became Christians. In just over 50% of the cases, the primary reason for conversion was intellectual. These former atheists mentioned that by studying subjects such as cosmology and intelligent design, and various philosophical arguments, they became convinced of the inherent rationality of Christianity.[15] Many scientists have also come to God after pondering the ultimate meaning of what they study. Among them is astrophysicist Chandra Wickramasinghe, who states: "From my earliest training as a scientist, I was very strongly brainwashed to believe science cannot be consistent with any kind of deliberate creation. That notion has been painfully shed. At the moment I can't find any rational argument to knock down the view that argues for conversion to God . . . Now we realize the only logical answer to life is creation—and not accidental random shuffling."[16] Christians know that God created the twin miracles of the universe and life, but regardless of an individual scientist's religious convictions, he or she cannot stop and simply conclude that God did it. We know that He did by "devising the rules of the game," as Nobel laureate physicist Erwin Schrodinger said. But Schrodinger also said that God left it up to science "to discover or to deduce."[17]

In Romans 1:20, Paul is saying that we can know at least *something* about God's invisible qualities by looking at His visible creation and pondering upon it. This sentiment is reflected in America's favorite worship song, *How Great Thou Art*: "Oh Lord, my God, when I, in awesome wonder, consider all the works Thy hands have made, I see the stars, I hear the rolling thunder, thy power throughout the universe displayed." Scripture urges us to behold the heavens and all the wonders therein so that we may recognize God in them. "Lift up your eyes and look to the heavens: Who created all these? He who brings out the starry host one by one and calls forth each of them by name. Because of his great power and mighty strength, not one of them is missing" (Isaiah: 40:26). We cannot fail to see that the universe proclaims a supreme intelligence that we Christians call God. As Albert Einstein has said: "Everyone who is seriously involved in the pursuit of science becomes convinced that a spirit is manifest in the laws of the Universe—a spirit vastly superior to that of man, and one in the face of which we with our modest powers must feel humble."[18] Science was in its infancy when Hume wrote about his "firm and unalterable experience," but from this firm and unalterable experience science has revealed to us miracles that he would classify as "impossible" based on the mind-frying improbabilities with which we are confronted.

Sproul, Lindsley, and Gerstner maintain that natural theology is only important for knowing that God exists, and knowing that God exists is the only thing that proves miracles:

> Natural theology shows that there is a God. If there is a God, miracles are possible. If a God exists who created the world and operates it, there can be no doubting that He can modify His modus operandi. On the other hand, if we did not know that there is a God, we would have to step into an irrational view of the operation of nature by chance. . . .. miracles cannot prove God. God, as a matter of fact, alone can prove miracles. That is, only on the prior evidence that God exists is a miracle even possible.[19]

I maintain that the evidential power runs both ways: the existence of God proves miracles and miracles, whether they be the miracles of the Bible or of science, provide evidence for His existence. Physicist Brandon Carter provides us with the concept of the Strong Anthropic Principle (SAP), which says: "The universe (and thus the fundamental parameters on which it depends) must be such as to admit the creation of observers within it at some stage"[20] SAP takes note of the many astonishing coincidences between different branches of physics that work together against mind-boggling odds to make intelligent life possible. Carter's statement strongly implies purpose and deliberate design behind the universe. Some powerful force must have been *miraculously* inserting new energy into the system from the moment of creation to allow for an anthropically-centered biocentric outcome. If atheists recoil at the notion of a purposeful universe, note that no less a mind than Albert Einstein believed in one: "The religious inclination lies in the dim consciousness that dwells in humans that all nature, including the humans in it, is in no way an accidental game, but a work of lawfulness that there is a fundamental cause of all existence."[21] There is no other reasonable explanation of why the universe had to "admit the creation of observers within it at some point;" an endless trail of astronomically improbable "happy accidents" just won't cut it.

Although we won't go any further than this one paragraph into it, scientists have applied statistics to revealed theology (mostly the prophecies centering around Jesus' birth, death, and Resurrection) as well as natural theology. Astrophysicist Hugh Ross informs us that 2,000 prophecies appearing in the Old Testament were fulfilled in the New Testament and notes: "Since the probability for any one of these prophecies having been fulfilled by chance averages less than one in ten (figured very conservatively) and since the prophecies are for the most part independent of one another, the odds for all these prophecies having been fulfilled by chance without error is less than one in 10^{2000} (that is 1 with 2,000 zeros written after it)!"[22] This fulfillment brings to mind Acts 3:18: " But those things, which God before had shewed by the mouth of all his prophets, that Christ should suffer, he hath so fulfilled."

Notes

1. In Fogelin, R., 1990, p. 82.
2. Craig, W., 1985, p. 480.
3. Ibid., p. 486.
4. Ibid., p. 487.
5. Ibid., p. 485.
6. Mackie, J., 1982, pp. 19–20.
7. Plantinga, A., 2011, p.79.
8. Dembski, W., 2004, pp. 84-85.
9. Ross, H., 1993, p. 115.
10. Wolchover, N., 2018, p. 3.
11. Schulz, H., 2017, p. 17.
12. Ibid, p. 15
13. Collins, F., 2007, np.
14. Davies, P., 1983, p. ix.
15. Langston, J., Powers, H., & Facciani, M., 2019.
16. In Seckbach, J., and Gordon, R., 2009. pp. 343-344.
17. In Moore, W., 2015, p. 348.

18. In Jammer, M. 1999, pp. 86-87.
19. Sproul, Lindsley, & Gerstner 1984, p. 146.
20. Carter, B., 1974, p. 294.
21. In Isaacson, W. 2007, p. 20.
22. Ross, H., 2003, p.1.

Chapter 2

The Miraculous Impossible Universe

The Unnatural Standard Model of Particle Physics

If you want to embrace a miracle that comports with all the regularities of human experience that Hume mentions, you are living in one—our impossible but inevitable universe. The instant appearance of mass and energy and the laws that govern it from nothing is the inaugural miracle that made all others possible. The discovery of the Higgs boson (a fundamental particle that established the existence of the Higgs field that imparts mass on other particles) in 2012 capped 50 years of an uninterrupted streak of successes for the Standard Model of particle physics that classifies and describes the behavior of all elementary particles. Such success notwithstanding, physicist Harry Cliff tells us that physicists regard the Standard Model as highly "unnatural" because of the large number of particles and forces that are so precariously balanced such that changing any of the values: "you rapidly find yourself living in a universe without atoms. This spooky fine-tuning worries many physicists, leaving the universe looking as though it has been set up in just the right way for life to exist."[1] Yes, we confront the miraculous here.

What does Cliff mean by calling the most successful model in science unnatural? Naturalness in physics is basically the prohibition against fine-tuning. If a theory requires the tweaking of its parameters in order to agree with experimental observation, it is considered "unnatural." The Higgs boson has such a lot of unnaturalness about it that Euan McLean says has led some physicists to panic about its "spooky" nature. The problem is that its mass is fine-tuned by multiple trillions of degrees more than the Standard Model predicted. That is, the actual measured mass (m) differs dramatically from its theoretical, or "bare" mass (m_0). As McLean points out: "The universe would be radically different if that value of m_0 was changed even a tiny bit.... It seems like, to generate a universe remotely like the one we live in, nature needs to decide on a parameter m_0, highly tuned to 33 decimal places."[2]

A fine-tuned universe is only spooky if one is committed to material nature as the only reality. Particle physicist Michael Strauss is not one of them and asks if the discovery of the Higgs boson provides us with insights into the existence and nature of God. He marvels at the fact that six physicists sat down in 1964 and came up with mathematical calculations that predicted the Higgs particle should exist, and then 48 years later it was discovered. The fact that we can describe the universe mathematically and can trust math to predict things about the universe, leads Strauss to opine that all explanations other than God are inadequate to explain our incredibly complex universe. He notes of the Higgs particle: "Though it may not be properly 'The God Particle,' the mathematical description and complexity of our universe, along with its actual existence, gives a clear indication of a true deity who has designed and created what we now have the privilege to observe and study."[3]

How miraculous is it that we have a universe we are privileged to observe and study? The most remarkable fine-tuning of all is getting the whole thing started. The issue of the state of the universe at the moment of creation is intimately connected to the second law of thermodynamics and entropy. Entropy means that any system becomes disordered without energy from outside the system; entropy always increases in a closed system. The universe is a closed system that will eventually arrive at maximum entropy. If the universe had always existed, it would have long ago entered a state of thermodynamic equilibrium. Increasing entropy is evident in the cosmic microwave background (CMB) radiation (remnant heat from the Big Bang) which is detected everywhere in the universe. From the multiple trillions of degrees at the Big Bang, the CMB now has a uniform temperature of 2.725° above absolute zero Kelvin, or -454.765° F. Heat continuously flows from hotter to colder environments until it is the same across the universe. This is thermodynamic equilibrium; zero degrees Kelvin—heat death.

Given this, there had to be an exquisite fine-tuning of the mass-energy distribution and the degree of order in the very beginning because a universe capable of supporting life must begin with the lowest possible entropy. Nobel laureate physicist Sir Roger Penrose asks us to imagine all the possible ways that the universe might have started and the probability that the Creator could hit the exact point to create a life-producing universe: "How big was the original phase-space volume W that the Creator had to aim for in order to provide a universe compatible with the second law of thermodynamics and with what we now observe?" He then remarks on two ways to estimate this figure and writes: "Either way, the ratio of V [total phase-space volume available] to W will be, closely $V/W = 10^{10^{(123)}}$."[4] This absurdly low number is many orders of magnitude beyond the probability boundary. It may be justly characterized as miraculous (mathematically "impossible") even as the universe's existence fully comports with David Hume's "regularities of experience."

Penrose notes that this number could not be written down if we had every elementary particle in the universe to write a zero on. Penrose's calculations present problems for atheists who have wrestled with the initial entropy problem themselves, as evidenced by a paper written by three distinguished physicists titled "Disturbing Implications of a Cosmological Constant." They noted that it is a given that the universe could only make sense if it began in a state of minimum entropy, and add: "there is no universally accepted explanation of how the universe got into such a special state...Far from providing a solution to the problem, we will be led to a disturbing crisis."[4] What is this disturbing crisis they found after examining all naturalistic explanations for such exquisite fine-tuning and finding them wanting? According to the authors, it is no less than forcing physicists to think the unthinkable: "Another possibility is an unknown agent intervened in the evolution, and for reasons of its own restarted the universe in the state of low entropy characterizing inflation."[5] The "unknown agent" they fear to name is God.

The Big Bang

Prior to the early 1930s, the standard position of science was that the universe is past eternal, static, and uncaused. This was a convenient position because it relieved scientists of having to ponder the question of its origin. Science now knows the universe had a beginning but is in a quandary regarding how or why it began, and the theistic implications of even thinking about it, but the Judeo/Christian view has always asserted a beginning as revealed in Genesis *1:1:* "In the beginning God created the heavens and the earth." God's creation was *creatio ex nihilo* ("creation from nothing"). Science had difficulty accepting this because it is a given that nothing (no-thing) can come *naturally* from nothing. Creation was God's first intervention outside Himself, and an action that could not have been caused by the laws of nature since the laws themselves came from the creation event. We may thus call the creation event the first miracle.

The Resurrection of Christ may be the greatest of miracles in terms of human eschatology, but something from nothing has to be the greatest miracle because things that come to an end must first have a beginning. It is now accepted science that the universe came into existence with the Big Bang some 13.8 billion years ago, at which time the laws of physics break down. If the laws of physics cannot supply an explanation due to this impasse, then the explanation must be beyond physics; that is, it must be *meta*physical. It is important to realize that the Big Bang is the beginning of the universe and not its cause; that was God's doing.

It was Belgian priest and mathematician-physicist, Georges Lemaître, who noted in the early 1920s that all was not right with a past-eternal static universe, reasoning that in a state of past eternity gravity would have long ago pulled all matter in the universe together into one huge mass. Lemaître drew the conclusion that to avoid this crunch the universe had to be expanding, and if it was expanding, it had to do so from a finite point in time. He reasoned that if the universe was expanding, rewinding of the cosmic clock should arrive at a point when all matter was condensed into a single entity, which he called the "primeval atom." Modern physicists call this the singularity; a "point" of almost infinite density and temperature. Everything that exists in the universe, every last atom, every physical force, and space/time itself was contained in this super-dense concentration of energy. This singularity was not some tiny dot hanging around in space somewhere because there was no "somewhere" for it to be, nor was it hanging around waiting to pop into existence because there was no time before it popped. The massive energy of the universe's inflation had to be exquisitely matched to its gravitational power such that if the rate of expansion from the beginning differed more than 10^{-18} seconds we wouldn't be here.[6]

It is not just starting with the lowest possible entropy or the matching of the explosive force with the force of gravity we must consider. Allen and Lidström inform us: "If the Standard Model were strictly obeyed, there should have been an essentially complete annihilation of matter and antimatter in the early Universe, leaving only photons." Matter consists of atoms with a negatively charged electron; antimatter contains a positively charged positron. When they come together there is mutual destruction, but that didn't happen. They called this a fundamental problem and "an extreme and unnatural fine-tuning in the initial state of the Universe."[7] Again, if something is unnatural it must be supernatural, and if it is supernatural, it is miraculous.

Early Opposition to the Big Bang

There was much initial opposition to the "spooky" implications of the Big Bang, both because it violated the long-held idea of a universe without a beginning and because it smacked too much of the Book of Genesis. As astrophysicist Robert Jastrow pointed out: "This religious faith of the scientist is violated by the discovery that the world had a beginning under conditions in which the known laws of physics are not valid, and as a product of forces or circumstances we cannot discover. When that happens, the scientist has lost control. If he really examined the implications, he would be traumatized."[8] And traumatized they were.

Georges Politzer noted what the Big Bang implied for materialism: "The universe was not a created object. If it were, then it would have to be created instantaneously by God and brought into existence from nothing. To admit Creation, one has to admit, in the first place, the existence of a moment when the universe did not exist, and that something came out of nothingness. This is something to which science cannot accede."[9] Allan Sandage, perhaps the greatest cosmologist of the 20th century, concluded: "It is such a strange conclusion....it cannot really be true." But upon pondering further, Sandage became a Christian, noting that "It was my science that drove me to the conclusion that the world is much more complicated than can be explained by science. It was only through the supernatural that I can understand the mystery of existence."[10] One scientist who accepted it from the beginning is Nobel laureate physicist Arno Penzias, who stated: "The best data we have (concerning the big bang) are exactly what I would have predicted had I nothing to go on but the five books of Moses, the Psalms, the Bible as a whole."[11] The Bible has always told us that the universe had a beginning and a cause, and that cause has to be an entity that transcends time, space, and matter/energy since these things did not exist before creation. Science only arrived at the truth about 100 years ago that the universe had a beginning. As astronomer George Greenstein wrote about the Big Bang: "As we survey all the evidence, the thought insistently arises that some supernatural agency, or rather Agency, must be involved. Is it possible that suddenly, without intending to, we have stumbled upon scientific proof of the existence of a Supreme Being?"[12]

Other Miraculous Facts About the Universe

Physicist Freeman Dyson once wrote: "As we look out into the Universe and identify the many accidents of physics and astronomy that have worked together to our benefit, it almost seems as if the Universe must in some sense have known that we were coming."[13] A universe that somehow knew we were coming implies an anthropic purpose for its being. The regularities observed around us are evidence of purpose or intention, but inanimate matter does not have intelligence or purpose, so the purposes and functions they exhibit must originate in an intelligent entity that devised their purpose via the laws of nature.

Among the many aspects of the universe that seem contrived is the contrast and density of matter that had to be just right from the first second of creation. Too much matter and the gravitational pull would be greater than the expansive force of the Big Bang causing it all to collapse back on itself; too little and the gravitational pull would be insufficient for matter to coalesce into stars and planets. This is known as the energy density of matter (p). There is a critical value (p_{crit}) of the energy density that prevents gravity from overcoming the force of expansion and pulling all matter into a big crunch. The value of p has to be microscopically close to p_{crit} to avoid this, and it had to vary by less than one part in 10^{60} from the very beginning of creation. Paul Davies expresses his amazement at this fine-tuning: "We know of no reason why p is not a purely arbitrary number... to choose p so close to p_{crit}, fine-tuned to such stunning accuracy, is surely one of the great mysteries of cosmology."[14]

The explosive force of the Big Bang was enough to balance out gravity for a long time, but this is slowly dissipating, thus requiring another force to prevent a "big crunch." The Supernova Cosmology Project began in 1998 expecting to measure the deceleration of the universe but found that it was actually accelerating. Gravity needed to dominate during the period of matter accretion into galaxies, stars, and planets, but for some reason known only to God, dark energy now rules the roost. Einstein's cosmological constant (the energy built into the vacuum of space—dark energy) has taken on the job of keeping the universe expanding. There is much about the amazing precision of the cosmological constant that puzzles the best minds in physics. Alejandro Jenkins and Gilad Perez remark that "the most serious fine-tuning problem in theoretical physics: the smallness of the 'cosmological constant,' thanks to which our universe neither recollapsed into nothingness a fraction of a second after the big bang, nor was ripped apart by an exponentially accelerating expansion."[15]

Physicists Livio and Rees inform us that anthropic reasoning is becoming seriously discussed in physics and may have predictive power for explaining phenomena such as the miraculous mystery of the cosmological constant. They ask: "Why is the force so small? If there was an inflationary era with a large cosmic repulsion, how could that force have been switched off (or somehow have been neutralized) with such amazing precision? In our present universe, Λ ['lambda;' the symbol for the cosmological constant] is lower by a factor of about 10^{120} than the value that seems natural to theorists."[16] The "switching off" or "neutralization" of repulsion Livio and Rees refer to must be unbelievably fine-tuned to 120 decimal places from the very beginning of the universe. Livio and Rees go on to note that: "If Λ were larger, then the acceleration would have overwhelmed gravity before galaxies had a chance to form."[17] Nobel laureate physicist Steven Weinberg exclaimed about the razor's edge balance between dark energy and gravity: "This is the one fine-tuning that seems to be extreme, far beyond what you could imagine just having to accept as a mere accident."[18]

Gravity is itself extraordinarily fine-tuned. Physicist Robin Collins asks us to imagine a gravity dial broken down into one-inch increments that stretch right across the universe. This would be more inches than all the grains of sand on Earth. Collins noted that if we moved gravity's setting just one inch out of those unimaginable trillions from its current setting, it would increase gravity by a billion-fold. If some malevolent finger moved the dial even the tiniest fraction of an inch to increase its power, everything in the universe would be crushed into a super-dense mass.[19] If, on the other hand, the dial was moved in the other direction reducing gravity by as little as 5%, the gravitational force holding the Earth's interior together would be weaker. This reduced force would result in numerous earthquakes, volcanos, and tsunamis, cloaking the Earth with layers of mushy volcanic ash. The weaker gravitational pull of the Sun on the Earth would move the Earth to a more distant orbit, resulting in less heat reaching us. The Sun would also cool down since it needs the crush of gravity to push hydrogen atoms to its core where they fuse together to release heat energy. The combination of the accumulation of ice and ash resulting from all these catastrophic events would eventually turn the Earth into a giant snowball. We can thank God that the gravity dial is miraculously set just right.

The Sun

Our Sun is not just any old star but rather one—and perhaps the only one—that has all the necessary characteristics to make complex life possible. Unlike about 85% of other stars, the Sun is solitary. The other 85% are locked with two or more other stars, which results in wild gravitational pulls that make stable planetary orbits impossible. The Sun's energy makes life possible by sending us its precious photons. When atoms are smashed together in the Sun's core, energy is released in the form of photons. In making these photons, the Sun consumes 600 million tons of hydrogen and turns it into 596 million tons of helium every second. The four million tons of mass lost is the energy (photons) produced by fusion. Sunlight is used as energy by plant life to synthesize foods from carbon dioxide and water in the process of photosynthesis.

The Sun has so many fine-tuned anthropic qualities that we cannot possibly get into here, but because of its many life-giving properties, some ancient civilizations worshiped the Sun as a god. Of course, the Sun is only a giant ball of hot gas, and unlike God, it had a beginning in time and will eventually die. Yet the Bible is chock-full of metaphorical references to the Sun, the light of our lives. For instance, Psalm 84:11 states: "For the Lord God is a sun and shield." We take this allegorically to mean that but for the love of God that enlightens, guides, and directs us, we would walk in darkness. Just as the physical Sun provides light, warmth, and beauty for us, the personhood of God is the source of light, joy, and happiness, for our souls; the light of the world that dispels darkness. God is also a shield of faith against the dark temptations of the flesh. Also like the Sun, God is distant, but we feel His rays like we feel the Sun's. Like the Sun when it shines on the other side of the Earth, God is there even when we can't see him are can't look directly at him. G.K. Chesterton said it best: "God is like the sun, you cannot look at it but without it you cannot look at anything else." Another great British writer, C.S. Lewis, likewise declared, "I believe in Christianity as I believe that the Sun has risen, not only because I see it but because by it, I see everything else."

There are hundreds of other unimaginably fine-turned to make our universe possible. I cannot say that I've "just scratched the surface." In fact, I've barely even dusted the surface so that I can scratch it. The necessary conditions for a universe fit for intelligent life are so many that astrophysicist Hugh Ross estimates that the probability of a planet falling within the necessary parameters for intelligent life as less than 1 in 10^{215}: "fewer than a trillionth of a trillionth of a percent of all stars will have a planet capable of sustaining advanced life. Considering that the observable universe contains less than a trillion galaxies, each averaging a hundred billion stars, we can see that not even one planet would be expected, by natural processes alone, to possess the necessary conditions to sustain life."[20]

Astrophysicist John Gribbin asks if intelligent life elsewhere in the universe and answers: "Almost certainly no, given the chain of circumstances that led to our existence."[21] On being awarded the prestigious Leonard Award for outstanding contributions to planetary science, Stuart Taylor addressed the difficulties of making an Earth-like planet given the staggering improbabilities of a myriad of things from the formation of the Milky Way to the origin of life and concluded: "When the remote chances of developing a habitable planet are added to the chances of both high intelligence and a technically advanced civilization, the odds of finding 'little green men' elsewhere in the universe decline to zero."[22] Astrobiologists Plaxco and Gross also weighed the probability of intelligent life on other planets given the multitude of exquisitely coordinated parameters required to get it going and concluded: "The range of values in Drake's parameters [an equation for estimating the probability of intelligent life beyond Earth] could adopt is so great, that despite the huge numbers of stars in the Universe, current scientific knowledge is entirely consistent with N=1. That is, Fermi [Enrico Fermi, the Italian-American Nobel Prize-winning physicist] was right, and we are alone."[23]

Of course, it really doesn't matter if our planet is unique. God could have literally salted the universe with intelligent life if that was his desire. His existence hardly rests on an affirmative answer to the question of human cosmic uniqueness. If against all odds intelligent life does exist elsewhere in the cosmos, why would that argue against His existence rather than for His creative power? Why should more be less? What we are witnessing as science advances is well-put by Nobel Prize-winning physicist Joseph J. Thomson: "As we conquer peak after peak we see in front of us regions full of interest and beauty, but we do not see our goal, we do not see the horizon; in the distance tower still higher peaks, which will yield to those who ascend them still wider prospects, and deepen the feeling, the truth of which is emphasized by every advance in science, that 'Great are the Works of the Lord.'"[24]

Think about this: We are compounds of molecules composed of two or more elements. Elements are atoms; atoms are composed of smaller particles .... and so on until at the lowest level the solidity of matter fades away into the vibrations of little strings of energy. What is behind those energy vibrations that are the rock bottom of natural reality? Nobel laureate Max Planck noted that these vibrations hold the atom together and concluded: "We must assume behind this force is the existence of a conscious and intelligent Mind. This Mind is the matrix of all matter."[25] Another great physicist, James Jean, has written: "Mind no longer appears to be an accidental intruder into the realm of matter... we ought rather hail it as the creator and governor of the realm of matter."[26] There are many other hard-headed physicists, including Nobel winners, who think of the universe as a great thought. What does that remind you of? "In the beginning was the Word, and the Word was with God, and the Word was God" (John 1.1).

Atheist Response: The Multiverse

Nobel laureate chemist Richard Smalley captured my position on our miraculous universe exactly when he wrote: "The purpose of this universe is something that only God knows for sure, but it is increasingly clear to modern science that the universe was exquisitely fine-tuned to enable human life. We are somehow critically involved in His purpose. Our job is to sense that purpose as best we can, love one another, and help Him get that job done."[27] This is unacceptable to atheists who, quite aware of the immense improbabilities of the universe's fine-tuning, have turned to speculations about a multiverse. If you don't want God, posit a multiverse, because either a fine-tuned universe has a fine-tuner, or else we have a multiverse of untold trillions of universes in which every possible combination of physical constants and forces exist somewhere; even one in which Hillary Clinton is president! The argument is that if there is an infinity of universes at least one should contain all the "coincidences" that have led to complex and intelligent life on Earth. This is like saying that if you buy all the lottery tickets you are bound to win the lottery.

The theory behind the multiverse is M-theory, which is purely mathematical and contains not one scintilla of empirical evidence. Alan Lightman concedes that we have no conceivable way of observing other universes and cannot prove their existence, but says: "Not only *must* we accept that the basic properties of our universe are accidental and incalculable. In addition, we *must* believe in the existence of many other universes... Thus, to explain what we see in the world and in our mental deductions, we *must* believe in what we cannot prove."[28] Lightman sounds like atheism's pope speaking *ex-cathedra* and demanding that all devout atheists must believe in an unseen and unknowable multiverse. Tim Radford captures nicely the God-like nature with which M-theory has been endowed: "M-theory invokes something different: a prime mover, a begetter, a creative force that is everywhere and nowhere. This force cannot be identified by instruments or examined by comprehensible mathematical prediction, and yet it contains all possibilities. It incorporates omnipresence, omniscience and omnipotence, and it's a big mystery. Remind you of Anybody?"[29] M-theory proposes a metaphysical entity we cannot know to replace one we can.

Cosmologist Bernard Carr finds it: "not surprising that the multiverse proposal has commended itself to atheists. Indeed, Neil Manson has described the multiverse as 'the last resort for the desperate atheist.' For if ours is the only universe, then one has a problem explaining the fine-tunings and might well be forced into a theological direction."[30] It is not only theistic scientists who criticize the multiverse hypothesis, however. Nobel laureate physicist, Richard Feynman, dismissed M-theory as "crazy," "nonsense," and "the wrong direction" for physics.[31] Ellis and Silk note that the mathematical elegance of M-theory generates grand but untestable hypotheses, and conclude: "theoretical physics risks becoming a no-man's-land between mathematics, physics and philosophy that does not truly meet the requirements of any."[32] They also argue that M-theory harms physics when proponents argue for relaxing the criteria by which a theory is judged useful or not, and note that among the time-honored criteria for a scientific theory is that it must be falsifiable. It is indeed strange to appeal to an unknowable to account for features of the universe we observe. Yet because M-theorists are faced with fundamental difficulties in meshing their theories to the observed universe have argued for a change in how physics is done.

Frank Tipler took a different route after pondering the fine-tuning of the universe: "When I began my career as a cosmologist some twenty years ago, I was a convinced atheist. I never in my wildest dreams imagined that one day I would be writing a book purporting to show that the central claims of Judeo-Christian theology are in fact true, that these claims are straightforward deductions of the laws of physics as we now understand them. I have been forced into these conclusions by the inexorable logic of my own special branch of physics."[33] The multiverse may be "the last resort for the desperate atheist," but even if it exists beyond the mathematical equations, it provides no comfort for the atheist because it still needed a Creator.

Atheist Response: Who Made God?

A favorite atheist philosophical response to Christian claims that God created the universe is "Who made God?" This is a meaningless question because only things that *begin to exist* have a cause. God is not bound by the naturalistic parameters of time, space, beginning, and causality—He is the beginningless Uncaused Cause. Thomas Aquinas' argument from causality addressed this centuries ago. Everything that begins to exist has a cause beyond itself which, in turn, has its own cause stretching far into the past. This chain of cause and effect cannot logically go on forever, so there must be an uncaused cause that causes all other things. Unless we assume there is a first uncaused cause we will be bedeviled by the problem of infinite regress, so there must be a logical terminus for caused events. After all, the universe is finite, so we can't keep pushing contingent causes back forever; we have to stop at something that is a sufficient explanation for its own existence. When we assert that everything is caused; we mean that everything *contingent*, everything *material*; everything in *time*, and everything *imperfect* requires a cause. The unconditional, immaterial, timeless, and perfect God does not. God is God precisely because He does not have a creator. He exists in and of Himself, independent of anything else. This is the *aseity* (the "of oneself") of God.

Another argument that addresses the infinite regress problem is Aquinas' argument from motion. This is an argument about change; things moving from a potential state to an actual state. The potential is something that does not exist as yet because it requires something else to actualize it. Whatever actualizes that potential must be actualized by something else and that something else must itself be actualized. This chain cannot be infinitely long, so there must exist some unchanged and unchanging entity that puts all change in motion. This points to the need for a power capable of causing all the changes in the universe from the beginning of time. We call this power God, the Unmoved Mover; the Changeless One.

If an atheist wants to stop the infinite regress of causes and changes with the universe as a self-created brute fact, he would have to assert that while it is true that everything manifest in the universe has a cause, the universe itself requires no explanation because it is the uncaused cause of itself (now, it seems, some scientists *do* want to say that nothing causes something). The atheist's universe pulled itself up by its own bootstraps and did it so astoundingly well that it produced intelligent beings capable of probing its secrets. To say that the universe is self-existent is analogous to saying that a man can literally be the father of himself, or a man can exist without being fathered. An "omnipotent" but mindless universe takes us back to the pre-1930s world in which the universe was considered a past eternal brute fact, and thus we need not bother ourselves pondering its origin. Rather than claiming that matter and energy somehow always existed or created itself, Nobel laureate physicist Sir Edmund Whittaker says: "It is simpler to postulate creation *ex nihilo*—Divine Will constituting Nature from nothingness."[34] The atheist has neither a natural nor a supernatural explanation for creation, which underlines the hollowness of his arguments—nothing created something from nothing for no reason!

Notes

1. Cliff, H., 2013, np.
2. McLean, E., 2017, np.
3. Strauss, M., 2017, np.

4. Penrose, R., 2016, pp. 445-446.
5. Dyson, L., Kleban, M., and Susskind, L., 2002. p. 3.
6. Davies, P., 1984, p. 184.
7. Allen, R. and Lidström, S., 2016, p. 10.
8. Jastrow, R., 1981, p. 19.
9. In Yahya, H. 1999, p. 19.
10. In Strobel, L., 2004, p. 84.
11. In Schaefer, H., 2003, p. 49.
12. In Strobel, L., 2004, p. 189.
13. Dyson, F. 1979, p. 250.
14. Davies, P. 1982, p. 90.
15. Jenkins, A., & Perez, G., 2010, p. 44.
16. Livio, M., & Rees, M., 2005, p. 1022.
17. Ibid, p. 1022.
18. In Folger, 2008, np.
19. In Strobel, L., 2004, p. 161.
20. Ross, H. 1994, pp. 169-170.
21. Gribbin, J., 2018, p. 99.
22. Taylor, S. 1998, p. 327.
23. Plaxo, K. and Gross, M., 2006, p. 247.
24. In Singh, S., 2004, pp. 361-362.
25. In Olsen, B. 2013, p.382.
26. Jeans, J. 1930, p. 137.
27. In Gefter, A. 2008, p. 48.
28. Lightman, A., 2011, pp. 38-40.
29. Radford, T., 2010, np.
30. Carr, B., 2013, p. 168.
31. In Amaldi, U., 2015, p. 179.
32. Ellis, G., and Silk, J., 2014, p.321.
33. Tipler, F., 1994, preface p. i.
34. In Heeren, F., 2000, p. 121.

Chapter 3

The Miracle of Life

Life: Rising from Dead Matter

Another statistical impossibility is the existence of intelligent life. This Earth teems with life but it was once a barren rock. Materialism posits that life arose by chance from dead matter and uses the term *abiogenesis* for the evolution of inorganic to organic molecules. But what is the probability of getting a live-sustaining Earth by chance? Gonzalez and Richards calculate it to be 10^{180}: "This would mean that, even in a universe with 10^{11} stars per galaxy and 10^{11} galaxies, totaling 11^{22} available attempts, the chances of getting one such system would still be one chance in 10^{158}."[1] This is well outside the probability boundary, but by some miracle, we are here; so how did life arise? The leap from lifeless chemicals to living matter would require a set of random undirected molecules to arrange themselves in a very specific way because living things must possess two extremely complex systems for them to be characterized as such: metabolism and reproductive capacity. The challenge that origin of life researchers is confronted with is not only how inanimate matter could be transformed into what we call life, but also which of these systems came first. Before life existed, how did these things that are essential to all living systems, and produced only by them, come into being?

Cells must have a mechanism to draw energy from their environment to fuel their metabolism and be able to self-replicate according to the information provided by DNA. These necessary things are so interdependent and complex that it is impossible to imagine how they could arise in an unguided fashion. There is such a mountain of chicken-or-egg problems in abiogenesis research that Nobel laureate Francis Crick has stated that: "An honest man, armed with all the knowledge available to us now, could only state that in some sense, the origin of life appears at the moment to be almost a miracle, so many are the conditions which would have had to have been satisfied to get it going."[2]

Scientists typically invoke an immense period of time to explain life's origin. They were confident after the 1953 Miller-Urey experiment produced sludge containing five amino acids, the building blocks of proteins, that it was just a matter of time before life was produced in the lab. This optimism has slowly faded to pessimism. Even Urey later admitted that while he believes in abiogenesis, he does not do so by dint of evidence, but by faith: "All of us who study the origin of life find that the more we look into it, the more we feel that it is too complex to have evolved anywhere. But we believe as an article of faith that life evolved from dead matter on this planet. It is just that its complexity is so great, that it is hard for us to imagine that it did."[3] Nobel laureate in physiology/medicine, George Wald also relied on faith when he noted that life from non-life is either spontaneous chance or Divine creation, but ruled out the latter because: "We cannot accept that on philosophical grounds; therefore, we choose to believe the *impossible*: that life arose spontaneously by chance!"[4] Wald later became a deist after pondering the fitness of the universe for life and consciousness: "It has occurred to me lately—I must confess with some shock at first to my scientific sensibilities—that both questions might be brought into some degree of congruence. This is with the assumption that mind, rather than emerging as a late outgrowth in the evolution of life, has existed always, as the matrix, the source and condition of physical reality—that the stuff of which physical reality is composed is mind-stuff."[5] Christians call Wald's "mind-stuff" from which physical reality came "the Word of God."

Biophysicist Dean Kenyon published a book in 1969 saying that chemical evolution to biological evolution was not only possible but inevitable (after all, we *are* here), but after 30 years of attempting to determine how complex proteins (the gap between the amino acids that Miller and Urey found and proteins could be measured in light years) could self-organize naturally, Kenyon came to the conclusion: "We have not the slightest chance of a chemical evolutionary origin for even the simplest of cells. ...so, the concept of the intelligent design of life was immensely attractive to me and made a great deal of sense, as it very closely matched the multiple discoveries of molecular biology."[4] Kenyon later abandoned atheism for theism. Nobel laureate biochemist Christian de Duve agrees with Kenyon, writing: "If you equate the probability of the birth of a bacterial cell to that of the chance assembly of its component atoms, even eternity will not suffice to produce one for you."[5] Famous physicist Sir Fred Hoyle also agreed: "It is apparent that the origin of life is overwhelmingly a matter of arrangement by intelligent control. *Unintelligent natural selection is only too likely to produce an unintelligent result.*"[6]

Amino Acids to Proteins

There are many thousands of articles and books relating to the origin of life and the problem of getting from amino acids to proteins and DNA. I can only provide the briefest of outlines here, but it is the sense of the miraculous I want to convey. The first problem is getting from amino acids to proteins. Amino acids are monomers ("one part") that must bond together into large molecular chains called polymers ("many parts") to form functioning proteins in the process of polymerization. An amino chain forming in the prebiotic aqueous soup would be far more likely to break apart than to assemble. Chemists point out that there is no evidence that a primordial soup ever existed, but even if it did: "Polymerisation into RNA requires both energy and high concentrations of ribonucleotides [the building blocks of RNA]. There is no obvious source of energy in a primordial soup. Ionizing UV radiation inherently destroys as much as it creates."[7] Moreover, molecular chemist Steven Benner informs us that: "An enormous amount of empirical data have established, as a rule, that organic systems, given energy and left to themselves, devolve to give useless complex mixtures."[8] Unguided organic reactions in a pool of chemicals form a useless gooey tar. Benner lists a number of other paradoxes that "suggest that it is impossible for any non-living chemical system to escape devolution to enter the Darwinian world of the 'living.'"[9] But we are here, so the scientifically impossible is *miraculously* possible with the guiding hand of Fred Hoyle's Super Intellect which we call God.

Unguided polymerization runs afoul of the second law of thermodynamics. Because polymerized molecules have already reacted, they are at thermodynamic equilibrium. No further reactions can occur in a system in thermodynamic equilibrium because there is no free energy intrinsic to the system that would allow them. Free energy can only be supplied to a living system by a mechanism (metabolism) that can harvest energy from the environment to counteract the decaying effects of the second law; only then can the living system break free from its shackles. The problem is that a system must already be alive for it to possess such a mechanism.

Getting amino acids to polymerize and produce protein also runs into the chirality problem. Chirality essentially means "mirror-imaged" or "non-superimposable" Two amino acids that are alike in structure and function (they have the same carbon, hydrogen, oxygen, and nitrogen atoms) may also be distinct from each other because they are mirror images; as your hands are. One version is labeled D ("dextro") for right-handed, and the other L ("levo"). Your hands are identical, but you cannot fit your right hand into your left glove. Likewise, D and L amino acids will not bond because chemical reactions that drive our cells only work with molecules of the correct "handedness." When amino acids are found in nonliving material or synthesized in the lab, they come equally in D and L forms called a *racemic* or heterochirality, but a homochiral set of acids is necessary for building proteins. All amino acids must be left-handed, and all sugars (ribose) must be right-handed to produce DNA and RNA.

Given that the laws of nature always produce a racemic, what is the probability that even a short protein could form randomly from all left-handed monomers? Plaxco and Gross use a short chain of 189 acids and inform us that it "is highly improbable that a random chemistry could produce a polymer molecule that contained monomers of only one-handedness. To be precise, the probability of achieving homochirality in a 189-unit polymer from an equal-molar mixture of left- and right-handed monomers is 1 in 2^{189} (1 in 8×10^{56})!"[10] A 189-unit polymer is very short; many polymers are thousands of monomers long, making it even more unlikely. Fred Hoyle and Chandra Wickramasinghe went further to write about the probability of getting the 20 amino acids to line up correctly and of obtaining a suitable sugar backbone for DNA/RNA along with functioning enzymes. They concluded: "there are about two thousand enzymes, and the chance of obtaining them all in a random trial is only one part in $(10^{20})^{2000} = 10^{40,000}$, an outrageously small probability .... this simple calculation wipes the idea entirely out of court."[11]

The Cell and DNA

If probability wipes a naturalistic unguided origin of life entirely out of court, we are confronted with the miraculous. Bill Bryson tells us that each of the trillions of cells in our bodies is a miniature miracle, and that to even produce a basic yeast cell: "you would have to miniaturize about the same number of components as are found in a Boeing 777 jetliner and fit them into a sphere just 5 microns [0.00019685 inches] across; then somehow you would have to persuade that sphere to reproduce."[12] Of course, human cells are vastly more complex than that. Cells contain the DNA within them that make the proteins that make us. The cell's microscopically small and elegantly ordered domain contains the membrane that supervises what molecules enter and exit, and separating them is a gelatinous liquid called cytoplasm. At the heart of the cell is the nucleus containing the DNA that sends instructions to the "workers" (the ribosomes) via messenger RNA about what proteins to make. The enormity of DNA's information content is such that: "If the sequence were typed onto paper, at about 3,000 letters per page, it would fill 1 million pages of text."[13] The awesome complexity of DNA is the language in which God wrote the book of life. This universal codebook with its immense information content reads, interprets, and edits itself, and is the most perfect code in existence.

DNA is information, but the chemistry of the DNA molecules is the messenger, not the message. A message needs a physical messenger, but the message is abstract information that needs interpreting. Astrobiologist Sara Walker and astrophysicist Paul Davies developed a model in which they talk of the fine-tuning of information and note that if the pathway from chemistry to life is the result of "fixed dynamical laws, then (our analysis suggests) those laws must be selected with extraordinary care and precision, which is tantamount to intelligent design: it states that 'life' is 'written into' the laws of physics *ab initio* ["from the beginning"]. There is no evidence at all that the actual known laws of physics possess this almost miraculous property."[14] And physicist Werner Gitt observes that the question of "How did life originate?" is inextricably linked to the question "Where did the information contained in all those base sequences in the genetic code come from?"[15] Mathematician John Lennox is not at all surprised that information is fundamental to life, and states: "This proposal, that information be regarded as a fundamental quantity, has profound implications for our understanding of the universe. But it is not new, it has been around for centuries. In the beginning was the Word...all were made by Him."[16]

There is so very much about DNA that inspires wonder that we cannot get into, but I cannot leave without discussing the mystery of protein folding. After a protein is made from a long chain of L amino acids, it must be folded into one of the millions of different intricate three-dimensional patterns if it is to function as designed in its receptor cell. Denton, Marshall, and Legge tell us that: "It is more than anything else the complex hierarchic structure of the folds—their being composed of clearly defined substructures and submotifs combined together into what appear seemingly to be irregular complex hierarchic wholes, the sort of order which is so characteristic of that of a machine or artifact—which conveys the irresistible feeling that such forms *could not possibly be natural or lawful.*"[17] Allen and Lidström call the protein folding process a "profound mystery of seemingly impossible complexity," and say that it is "far beyond the ability of current computer simulations to replicate."[18] Efforts have been made to do so, however, using an IBM computer with immense computing power called Blue Gene. IBM scientists note that protein folding is: "a fundamental problem in science or engineering"... and that it will take "Blue Gene about a year to simulate on the computer the folding of a single protein. How long does it take the body to fold one? Less than a second. It is absolutely amazing the complexity of the problem and the simplicity with which the body does it every day."[19] If a computer capable of more than 1,000 trillion operations per second takes a year to simulate what our genomes do thousands of times each day in less than a second, what a miracle we are.

Carbon: It's Incredibly Improbable Existence

Carl Sagan once famously remarked that we are literally "made of star stuff." All elements in our bodies were forged in the stars, but carbon is paramount because all life is carbon-based. Carbon atoms form the backbone of millions of organic compounds and have 6 protons and 6 neutrons in their nuclei and 6 electrons swirling around them. The carbon atom has two electron shells, the inner one holding two electrons and the outer one holding four valence electrons. Valence electrons determine the number of other atoms with which an element can form covalent bonds (sharing of electrons between atoms) with others. Carbon has room to form 4 bonds with other elements, which will fill its outermost shell with the 8 electrons needed for stability. This configuration allows carbon to form an unparalleled number of bonds and is one of the few elements that can bond with itself. Furthermore, carbon bonds are formed and broken with very little energy, which easily facilitates the dynamic organic chemistry that occurs in our cells.

As with all elements beyond hydrogen and helium, carbon is produced by the stars and is the fourth most abundant element in the universe. Physicists were once puzzled by such abundance because most stars are thousands of times cooler than required to burn helium into carbon. Then Fred Hoyle came up with his prediction of the energy level needed for its stellar nucleosynthesis. Carbon is made when three alpha particles (the nuclei of helium) fuse their combined protons and neutrons to form carbon-12 (^{12}C). But "as soon as ^{12}C is synthesized from helium, it absorbs another α [alpha] particle and becomes ^{16}O [oxygen] leaving no carbon. The reaction forming ^{12}C was much slower than the reaction that destroys it. If so, argued Hoyle, life should not exist!"[20] Physicists John Gribbin and Martin Rees note that Hoyle reasoned from the fact that we exist to predict that carbon must have a certain resonant energy level, and that was precisely the level experiments found it to be, and add: "There is no better evidence to support the argument that the Universe has been designed for our benefit–tailor-made for man."[21]

To fuse two atomic nuclei requires the energy of incoming nuclei to resonate with the energy of the receiving nuclei in a process called resonance energy transfer. Two fused helium nuclei create a highly unstable isotope of beryllium which decays back into two helium nuclei in about 10^{-17} seconds (one ten-thousandth of a trillionth of a second); making carbon thus requires exquisite precision in timing. It is estimated only one in 2,500 fusions transition to stabilize carbon atoms, but even these are in danger if another alpha particle fuses with it to produce oxygen. We need oxygen, but we don't want it at the expense of carbon. Preventing that is their respective energy levels. A very slight change in the nuclear resonance levels of oxygen and carbon would make the production of carbon impossible.

Fred Hoyle remarked on this process: "If you wanted to produce carbon and oxygen in roughly equal quantities by stellar nucleosynthesis, these are the two levels you would have to fix, and your fixing would have to be just where these levels are actually found to be." He then tries to understand how it could have happened: "*A commonsense interpretation of the facts suggests that a super-intellect has monkeyed with physics, as well as with chemistry and biology, and that there are no blind forces worth speaking about in nature.* The numbers one calculates from the facts seem to me so overwhelming as to put this conclusion almost beyond question."[22] Who else but Almighty God could be the super-intellect that "monkeyed" with the laws of physics (carbon's improbable fusion), chemistry (its amazing bonding features), and biology (its basis for life)? Hoyle said that he believed that any scientist who examined the evidence would "draw the inference that the laws of nuclear physics have been deliberately designed with regard to the consequences they produce inside the stars. If this is so, then my apparently random quirks have become part of a deep-laid scheme. If not, then we are back again to a monstrous sequence of accidents."[23] Yet there are many who prefer to place their faith in a "monstrous sequence of accidents" than in a Divine Creator.

Theistic Evolution

Does all this mean that we can disavow evolution as some Christians maintain? Many Christians believe in theistic evolution (TE), also known as Creative Evolution. TE holds the belief that God created all living things using the process of evolution in ways that conform to scientific accounts, but it denies that it is undirected and purposeless. The logic of TE is that everything evolves, and that evolution simply means the gradual development of a thing from a simple to a more complex form. We have no argument with the evolution of the universe. From the flash of unimaginable energy spoken into being at the Big Bang, we had the evolution of fundamental particles, which evolved into protons, neutrons, and electrons, which evolved into atoms of hydrogen and helium. These simple gases then evolved into stars and planets. Our Earth is one of those planets that evolved from a barren rock to the complex matrix of life that it is today. TE asks that if God allowed the universe that we observe today to evolve from the pure energy of the Big Bang, why not life? We are after all undisputable "made of star stuff." For TE scientists, biological evolution is the disguised friend of theism because it, like the discoveries of cosmology, grants us insights into how God made us.

TE posits a creative self-organizing universe containing laws that made possible the existence of intelligent beings. It does not require a God who tinkers with his creation, but rather a God who allows the continuous unfolding of properties invested in nature from the moment of creation. God gives the material universe, so to speak, the same kind of freedom that He gives the immaterial human mind. TE is not saying that nature acts independently of God's direction, only independently of His *direct* and immediate control. Theologian Charles Kingsley captured the idea of TE when he wrote: "We knew of old that God was so wise that he could make all things: but behold, He is so much wiser than that, that he can make all things make themselves."[24] Another theologian, Mats Wahlberg, notes that humans can create but only God can create things able to create themselves: "If it takes more wisdom to create through an evolutionary process than by hands-on-design, and if structures created by hand-on-design by humans are expressive of human intent and intelligence, why could not structures created by God in that more wisdom-demanding way reflect divine intent and intelligence?"[25] TE is accepted by all mainstream Protestant denominations and by the Catholic Church, so it must have a strong persuasive punch.

Augustine's words in *Commentary on Genesis* (V.4:11) show that Darwinism is pretty old stuff: "It is therefore, *causally* that Scripture has said that earth brought forth the crops and trees, in the sense that *it received the power of bringing them forth*. In the earth from the beginning, in what I might call the roots of time, God created what was to be in times to come." Thomas Aquinas, writing in the 13th century, noted: "Nature is nothing but the plan of some art, namely a divine one, put into things themselves, by which those things move towards a concrete end: as if the man who builds up a ship could give to the pieces of wood that they could move by themselves to produce the form of the ship."[26] Both Augustine and Aquinas point out that the natural properties of the earth that make crops and trees possible are secondary to the primary cause immanent in the laws of nature from the very beginning of the universe. This is identical to Darwin's view: "To my mind it accords better with what we know of the laws impressed on matter by the Creator, that the production and extinction of the past and present inhabitants of the world should have been due to secondary causes…"[27] Darwin was no atheist, and he said so!

TE avers that God willingly surrenders some of his authority and grants nature the freedom to make itself by natural force as He grants us the power to make of ourselves what we will. Anglican priest and physicist John Polkinghorne writes: "The play of life is not the performance of a predetermined script, but a self-improvisatory performance by the actors themselves.… God shares the unfolding course of creation with creatures, who have their divinely allowed, but not divinely dictated, roles to play in is fruitful becoming."[28] Polkinghorne's God is constantly working creatively through the unfolding of the inherent potentialities in nature. This is also the position of Albertus Magnus, 13th century scientist, philosopher, and theologian: "In studying nature we have not to inquire how God the Creator may, as He freely wills, use His creatures to work miracles and thereby show forth His power; we have rather to inquire what Nature with its immanent causes can naturally bring to pass."[29]

The Miracle of You

The human body is the most complex information-processing system in the universe. We often express awe and wonder with many things without ever realizing that we are more worthy of wonder than any of them. We are stunningly engineered creations of interrelated functionality blessed with the

The Miracle of Life   33

ability to self-repair and to make others of our kind. The human body's interconnected systems are a miracle of mechanical and chemical engineering, converting food into energy and living tissue that repairs itself, and a million other things automatically every minute of every day. Physicist and information theorist Werner Gitt notes that if we take the conscious processes such as thought, speech, and deliberate voluntary movements, combined with unconscious automatically controlled processes: "this involves the processing of 10^{24} bits daily. This astronomically high figure is higher by a factor of 1,000,000 than the total human knowledge of 10^{18} bits stored in all the world's libraries."[30]

There are so many thousands of marvels in the human body that we cannot get into here. But let us just make a brief mention of the interconnected system of the heart, lungs, kidneys, and blood system, and the eyes. Biologist Brad Harrub notes of the circulatory system: "A close examination of this complex network reveals architectural planning and design that can only be comprehended in light of an intelligent Designer. Our extensive knowledge of the human circulatory system is tremendous evidence of the existence of Almighty God."[31] The circulatory system's pipelines (arteries, veins) laid out end-to-end would stretch to about 80,000 miles, and each cell of your body is serviced by it every 20 seconds.[32]

Eyes are our windows to the wonders of the universe. Photons of light bathe the universe, and we behold its wonders via a vast array of photoreceptors in the retina linked via the optic nerve that collects them. The optic nerves send the photons all the way to the occipital lobe at the rear of the brain which receives, organizes, and interprets the patterns they generate. Computer engineer John Stevens compares the ability of our eyes to a computer. Today's computing power is impressive, but it cannot begin to match the performance of the human retina. Stevens explains:

> Actually, to simulate 10 milliseconds (ms) of the complete processing of even a single nerve cell from the retina would require the solution of about 500 simultaneous nonlinear differential equations 100 times, and would take at least several minutes of processing time on a Cray supercomputer. Keeping in mind that there are 10 million or more such cells interacting with each other in complex ways, it would take a minimum of 100 years of Cray time to simulate what takes place in your eye many times every second.[33]

As Psalm 139:14 says: "I praise you because I am fearfully and wonderfully made; your works are wonderful, I know that full well."

Sitting on your shoulders is God's magnum opus; the brain. It is the most immensely complicated and awe-inspiring entity in the universe containing many thousands of physical mechanisms and chemical substances. The human brain is so complex that we may never understand it. As it has been said many times in neuroscience circles: If the human brain were so simple that we could understand it, we would be so simple that we couldn't. Nobel laureate in physiology and medicine Roger Sperry rhapsodized about the brain's complexity and mystery: "In the human head there are forces within forces within forces, as in no other cubic half-foot of the universe we know;"[34] and Nobel laureate physicist Sir Roger Penrose wrote that our brains are a tiny part of the cosmos: "But it is the most organized part. Compared to the complexity of the brain, a galaxy is just an inert lump."[35] We could exhaust a dictionary of metaphors to sing the praises of this enchanted loom because within its churning chemical soup and buzzing electrical sparks lie our thoughts, memories, desires, emotions, intelligence, and creativity. Everything we do engages the brain as its electrochemical circuitry captures our genetic dispositions and environmental experiences and blends them into a self-conscious human being.

The brain enables the mind to think, discover, create, and worship, but materialists view the immaterial mind as a mere epiphenomenon of the material brain. Materialism relegates the conscious mind to brain activity with no independent existence; "A computer made of meat," as some neuroscientists like to call it. Of course, we cannot think without a brain just as we cannot breathe without lungs. But lungs exist so that we may breathe, and brains exist so that we can "mind." Materialists get it backward; the mind is not the brain at work; rather, the brain is the mind at work. Humans seem naturally inclined toward materialism because we live in a material world and thus tend to think in terms of space and form, and with stuff that we can see, hear, taste, and touch. The immaterial realm, on the other hand, is rarely thought about, and when it is, many are inclined to dismiss it. Yet no one has the slightest idea how anything material like the brain could be conscious of itself. Nobel laureate neuroscientist and brain surgeon Sir John Eccles rejects the notion of mind as an epiphenomenon of the brain and says:

> The more we discover scientifically about the brain the more clearly do we distinguish between the brain events and the mental phenomena and the more wonderful do the mental phenomena become. There is a fundamental mystery in my personal existence, transcending the biological account of the development of my body and my brain. That belief, of course, is in keeping with the religious concept of the soul and with its special creation by God.[36]

We are truly "fearfully and wonderfully made," and no less a miracle because we are commonplace or because science tells us the natural, albeit God-guided, way that we came to be. Science can tell us that tell us all about our bodies in minute details now that we are here, but not why life inhabits the universe in the first place. Based on the kind of information presented in this and the previous chapter, it is difficult not to agree with Nobel laureate physicist Joseph Taylor who notes: "There is no conflict between science and religion. Our knowledge of God is made larger with every discovery we make about the world."[37]

Notes

1. Gonzalez, G. & Richards, J., 2004, p. 327.
2. In Lim, R., 2017, p. 58.
3. In Persaud, C., 2007, p. 84.
4. Wald, G., 1954, p.48.
5. Wald, G., 1984, p.1.
6. Kenyon, D., 2002, p. 35.
7. Lane, N., Allen, J., & Martin, W., 2010, p. 272.
8. Benner, S., 2014, p. 341.
9. Ibid, p. 342.
10. Plaxco, K., & Gross, M., 2006, p. 114.
11. Hoyle, F., & Wickramasinghe, C., 1981, pp.19-21.
12. Bryson, B. 2003. p. 372.
13. Clark, D. & Pazdernik, N., 2009, p. 239.
14. Walker, S., & Davies, P., 2016, pp. 5-6.
15. Gitt, W., Compton, B. & Fernandez, J., 2011, p.169.
16. Lennox, J., 2009, p.177.
17. Denton, M., Marshall, C., & Legge, M., 2002, p. 339; emphasis added.
18. Allen, R. & Lidström S., 2016, p. 36.
19. IBM. 1999, np.
20. Shaviv, G. 2015, p. 311.
21. Gribbin, J. & Rees, M., 1989, p. 247.
22. Hoyle, F., 1982, p. 16; emphasis added.
23. In Holder, R., 2013, p. 48.
24. In Russell, R., 2008, pp. 167-168.
25. Wahlberg, M., 2012, p. 182.
26. Aquinas, T. 1963, p. 124.
27. Darwin, C., 1982, p. 458.
28. Polkinghorn, J., 2001, p. 94.
29. In Walsh, J., 2013, p. 338.
30. Gitt, W., 1996, p. 187.
31. Harrub, B. 2005. p. 82.
32. Nuland, S., 1997.
33. Stevens, J. 1985, p. 287
34. In Fincher, J., 1982, p. 23.

35. In Holt, J., 2018, p. 178.
36. In Alexander III, E., 2015, p. 20.
37. In Callaway, M., 2018, p. 19.

Chapter 4

The Atonement, Hell, and Universal Salvation

The Atonement

The Resurrection is the miraculous event that ushered in the New Covenant and cemented the atoning sacrifice of Christ. A very important issue in Christianity is whether the Atonement suggests limited or universal salvation. The Resurrection of Jesus Christ is inextricably linked with His Atonement for the sins of humanity. The meaning of the Atonement is succinctly given by Paul in Romans 5:18: "Consequently, just as one trespass [Adam's sin] resulted in condemnation for all people, so also one righteous act resulted in justification and life for all people." There is only one interpretation of the phrase "all people," and that is as it states: *all* people. However, the issue debated by conservative traditionalists and liberal universalists is: does that "all" really mean a truly inclusive all, or just all that portion of humanity that accepts the offer of the saving grace of Jesus Christ? Whatever the case may be, the Resurrection affirmed the promise of Atonement, and without Jesus' death on the cross, there would be no redeeming Resurrection. As H.D. McDonald explains:

> By means of the cross and empty tomb the salvation of God has become historical and eternal. Christ's atonement is historically absolute in the cross and eternally actual in the resurrection. ... Without the cross the resurrection might have been seen as a miracle but with no relation to men's lives, and without the resurrection the cross must have been seen as a mistake with no relation to their sin. Without the resurrection the cross cannot be understood as atoning, and without the cross the resurrection cannot be experienced as redeeming.[1]

In Exodus 1:37, God gave specific and detailed instructions to be followed for entering that part of the tabernacle called the Holy Place, at the back of which was a smaller chamber called the Holy of Holies. The Holy of Holies contained the Ark of the Covenant, and only the high priest could enter there and only on one day of the year. That special day was called the Day of Atonement. On that day the high priest, hidden behind a curtain, would sprinkle sacrificial blood on the Ark to symbolically atone for the sins of the people. The great secrecy of this event symbolized both God's holiness and His inaccessibility to the general population due to its sinful nature. This all changed when Jesus died and was resurrected: "At that moment the curtain of the temple was torn in two from top to bottom" (Matthew 27:51). And Hebrews 9:12 says that when Christ "entered once for all into the holy places, not by means of the blood of goats and calves but by means of his own blood, thus securing an eternal redemption."

The torn curtain symbolizes that the way to God was now not only open to the high priest, but open to all through the atoning death and Resurrection of Jesus Christ. "Therefore, brothers, since we have confidence to enter the holy places by the blood of Jesus, by the new and living way that he opened for us through the curtain, that is, through his flesh, and since we have a great priest over the house of God, let us draw near to God with a sincere heart and with the full assurance that faith brings." (Hebrews 10:19-22). Thus, in the greatest of all victories of hope over despair, God has conquered death through Jesus, and we can all enter God's presence. "Praise be to the God and Father of our Lord Jesus Christ! In his great mercy he has given us new birth into a living hope through the resurrection of Jesus Christ from the dead" (Peter 1:3).

Hell

Such good news is tempered by the threat of hellfire. The traditional view of hell is that of an unimaginably horrific place. This view is attributed to Augustine of Hippo (circa 354-430), grimly illustrated for us by Dante Alighieri (1265 – 1321) in his *Inferno*, and perhaps most hideously described by 18th-century American theologian and preacher Jonathan Edwards:

> Hell is a spiritual and material furnace of fire where its victims are exquisitely tortured in their minds and in their bodies eternally, according to their various capacities, by God, the devils, and damned humans including themselves, in their memories and consciences as well as in their raging, unsatisfied lusts, from which place of death God's saving grace, mercy, and pity are gone forever, never for a moment to return.[2]

Augustine's position is one held by most conservative theologians but it is a problem for more liberal theologians since it conflicts with the Christian idea of a loving and just God. In Edwards' Dantesque view, God not only allows eternal torture but practices it Himself. But eschatology speaks not only of humanity's destiny, but of the nature of God, and it is impossible to imagine that a loving and just God condemns the mass of His creation to perdition, much less participate in its torture. A deductive argument from what Christians maintain is the self-evident premise that God is loving, merciful, and just, and cannot logically arrive at the conclusion that God tortures or allows perpetual torture. Endless punishment defeats the demands of justice because the concept of justice is steeped in the concept of mercy. Justice without mercy and mercy without justice corrupt both concepts. Yet in Augustine's sadistic view of God, "he even argues that God can justly condemn those who die in infancy because they are all drawn from a corrupt mass."[3] Jesuit priest and professor of theology John Sachs abhors such views and disavows the traditional view of hell:

> [F]or many centuries, the doctrine of hell has had an exaggerated place in the theology and preaching of the Church. For many Christians, the 'good news' of the kingdom became the 'bad news' about judgment and punishment. Then, in reaction to the excessively juridical and often monstrous images of God which had been prevalent for so long, it has become common to ignore the topic of hell altogether or to deny its existence outright as incompatible with God's love and mercy.[4]

God told Adam in Genesis 2:17 that the penalty for breaking His law is death, not eternal torment. If God intended to send Adam and future sinners to a fiery hell, He surely would have said so. Who created hell? Certainly not God. Genesis 1.1 says: "In the beginning God created the heavens and the earth;" not a word about a place called hell. Many modern theologians note that the view that most souls will experience everlasting suffering is not embraced by those who believe that: "God's love must be maximally extended and equally intense."[5] The vast majority of people who ever lived were not Christians; they received whatever religious faith (if any) they had from their family and their culture, and was not freely chosen. It is a denial of God's all-embracing love to believe that those who have never even heard of Jesus must burn in hell for eternity. As John Hick asks: "Should we conclude that we who have been born within the reach of the gospel are God's chosen people, objects of a greater divine love than the rest of the human race? But then, on the other hand, do we not believe that God loves all God's creatures with an equal and unlimited love?"[6]

Even if one is "born within the reach of the gospel," most people live their lives without giving it much thought, just as they fail to give thought to most things. This does not mean that they reject Jesus any more than they reject the other things they fail to understand as they busy themselves with living. One must know something before accepting or rejecting it in any rational sense; we cannot reject that which we do not know, and we cannot know what has not been brought to our attention in ways that piqued our interest. Ignorance or indifference is not rejection, and people cannot be condemned for failing to explore what has not reached their consciousness in a forceful way. If I reject biological evolution, for instance, I must be well acquainted with it and provide strong epistemic reasons for rejecting it. Peter really knew Jesus but denied Him three times, but Jesus forgave him. If an informed rejection (albeit a temporary one) can be forgiven, why not an uninformed indifference?

Although I was never an atheist, science was my consuming intellectual passion. My journey to a greater knowledge of God began when I became aware of the persecution of Christian wedding vendors who refused to cater to same-sex weddings. I wrote an article on that topic, and then two books. Researching the topic piqued my interest in natural theology and this led me to explore revealed theology. Without that initial awareness, I may still be interested only in worldly matters, but I don't believe for a moment that it would mean I was removed from God's love. Even had I gone no further than my outrage over the persecution of Christian wedding vendors He would still love me. As Isaiah 54:8 says: "'In a surge of anger I hid my face from you for a moment, but with everlasting kindness I will have compassion on you,' says the Lord your Redeemer." And 2 Timothy 2:13 tells us: "If we are faithless, He remains faithful; He cannot deny Himself." A God who is forever angry with the faithless would make anger one of his "Omni" attributes, and this would negate his true omnibenevolent attribute.

Most people understandably cringe at the thought of people who basically lived good lives that die with a few peccadillos blotting their souls suffering the same fate as the monstrously evil. How could souls in Heaven ever rest content in the knowledge that their loved ones are suffering the eternal fires of hell, and perhaps for transgressions that would get them a short time in jail from an earthly judge? Surely God's justice is superior to human justice, and He surely punishes according to the light a person has received and what he or she does with it. The belief in a place of everlasting torment creates a religion of fear, coercing people to worship; sincerely or not. What then of people freely choosing to follow Christ? Good earthly fathers want their children to obey them out of love and respect, not out of fear, and our heavenly Father wants the same thing. The Church of England's Doctrine Commission expressed its horror of the traditional view of hell and offered its own view of the afterlife: "Christians have professed appalling theologies which made God into a sadistic monster. ... Hell is not eternal torment, but it is the final and irrevocable choosing of that which is opposed to God so completely and so absolutely that the only end is total non-being."[7] I wonder how many otherwise good people have turned their backs on Christianity when confronted with the "appalling theologies" of hell?

Paul tells us in Ephesians 3:11 that God had a definite purpose "accomplished in Christ Jesus our Lord" in mind before He created us. Given this, and given our belief in an omnibenevolent God, Gerald Bray asks "if the non-elect have no hope of salvation and God does not want them to suffer unduly, why were they ever created in the first place?"[8] Why indeed. Our image of God cannot conceive of Him as one who would create beings just to watch them suffer eternally for His heart is not cold. Faith is essential for the good Christian, but as 1 Corinthians 13:2 tells us, love is superior to faith: "If I have the gift of prophecy and can fathom all mysteries and all knowledge, and if I have a faith that can move mountains, but do not have love, I am nothing." And 1 Corinthians 13:13: "And now these three remain: faith, hope and love. But the greatest of these is love." Faith and hope apply only to oneself, but love entails service to others. Matthew 25:31-46 notes it is those who lovingly cared for the needs of the hungry, thirsty, naked, and imprisoned who will sit at God's right hand on Judgement Day. As I read these passages, faith matters, but it is not enough, and loving deeds matter most and form the basis of Divine judgment. Romans 13:8-10 tells us that love is the summation of all God's commandments and fulfills the Law:

> Let no debt remain outstanding, except the continuing debt to love one another, for whoever loves others has fulfilled the law. The commandments, "You shall not commit adultery," "You shall not murder," "You shall not steal," "You shall not covet," and whatever other command there may be, are summed up in this one command: "Love your neighbor as yourself." Love does no harm to a neighbor; therefore love is the fulfillment of the law.

Paul says if you love your neighbor, you will do them no wrong. You don't have to be a Christian believer to approach your neighbors with an active concern for their well-being. The passage from Romans implies that all good people of whatever belief system (or none at all) who do this are righteous and deserve God's mercy. It is doubtless easier to live a good life by faith in Christ, but millions of non-Christians, and even atheists, have fulfilled the law. As Romans 2:14-15 says: "Indeed, when Gentiles, who do not have the law, do by nature things required by the law, they are a law for themselves, even though they do not have the law. They show that the requirements of the law are written on their hearts, their consciences also bearing witness, and their thoughts sometimes accusing them and at other times even defending them." Thus, those who do not have the written law have the law of conscience to morally direct them. Romans 2:13 points out that persons without the law who follow their conscience are better persons than those who have the law but do not live it: "For it is not those who hear the law who are righteous in God's sight, but it is those who obey the law who will be declared righteous."

John Calvin and Predestination

The views of 16th-century French theologian John Calvin are worse even than those of Augustine or Edwards. Calvin argued that because God is omniscient, He knows everything you will do before you do it, and therefore your actions are predetermined. Central to Calvinism is the belief in predestination whereby some have been selected by God for salvation from all eternity, and all others are destined for eternal damnation. Calvin based this on Romans 9:15: "For he said to Moses, I will have mercy on whom I will have mercy, and I will have compassion on whom I will have compassion," which he interpreted to mean that there is nothing people can do can save themselves from damnation if they are not among the elect. There is no hope of salvation in the act of choosing God because God chose you before you were born for salvation or damnation. Calvin wrote: "Hence we maintain that, by his providence, not heaven and earth and inanimate creatures only, but also the counsels and wills of men are so governed as to move exactly in the course which he has destined."[9] If this is so, how can we be held accountable for sinful choices if we are destined to move as God has predetermined? How can God be love in this view, and why was the atoning sacrifice of Jesus Christ even necessary?

Calvinism avers that to assert that we are free moral agents who can choose Christ as savior is to deny our depravity. Man cannot avoid sin; his choices are only between a greater or lesser evil. Calvinism says that free will is an illusion: "Man is a free agent but he cannot originate the love of God in his heart. His will is free in the sense that it is not controlled by any force outside of himself. As the bird with a broken wing is 'free' to fly but not able, so the natural man is free to come to God but not able."[10] Adding to this dismal picture, Calvin wrote: "Men do nothing save at the secret instigation of God, and do not discuss and deliberate on anything but what he has previously decreed with himself, and brings to pass by his secret direction."[11] This is a God-of-the-gaps argument raised to the Nth power. Since Calvin's God is the author of every sinful act we perform—God did it! We are not responsible for our actions; not because of our genes and experiences, but because our deliberations and decisions are initiated by the "secret instigation of God." Such a fatalistic theology delivers Christianity into the hands of atheists who may proclaim that since God is the author and instigator of sin, He is not worthy of our love and devotion. However, a God who "is utterly indifferent to the fate of billions of rational creatures, is as far removed from the God of the New Testament as heaven is from hell itself."[12]

How can we reconcile God's omniscience with free will without traveling down Calvin's road? Perhaps God has surrendered part of His power to foresee future events (the concept of *kenosis*) brought about by free human actions since He has gifted us with that freedom. Even if this is not so, just because an omniscient God knows what you will do does not mean that He made you do it. Humans exist in the arrow of time in which there is a before, a now, and an after. God, however, is outside of time where there is no before or after; only an eternal now in which a human past, present, and future exist simultaneously: "I was, I am, I will be." God knew what you will do because He knows everything, but don't make God responsible for you doing it.

Universalist Eschatology

Theologian Richard Harries opines that if: "God knew from the beginning that some would, through their own choice, end up in intolerable torment, but he still went ahead and created the world. Such a god is a monster who would have to be rejected on moral grounds. The choice is clear. Either all will be saved or believe in a divine torturer, if you will."[13] If God condemned the vast majority of humanity to a literal hell leaving only those who love him to share His kingdom, it would be a pyrrhic victory coming at a cost God surely would not want to pay. It would seem that evil had won the day by forcing God to angrily destroy most of His creations. The eschatological alternative to a "divine torturer" is universal salvation. This position coheres with the loving and just nature of God and with this very short sample of the many scriptural verses supporting universal salvation:

Psalms 65:2: "All men will come to God."

2 Peter 3:9: "The Lord is not slow to fulfill his promise as some count slowness, but is patient toward you, not wishing that any should perish, but that all should reach repentance."

1 Timothy 2:4: "Whose will it is that all should find salvation."

Romans 11:32: "For God has consigned all to disobedience, that he may have mercy on all."

Colossians 1.20: "For in him God in all his fullness chose to dwell and through him to reconcile all things to himself."

Acts 3:21: "He must be received into the heaven until the time comes for the universal restoration of which God has spoken through his prophets from the beginning."

Titus 2:11: "For the grace of God has appeared, bringing salvation for all people."

Luke 3:6: "And all flesh shall see the salvation of God."

Revelation 5:13: All created beings in the universe will worship God and Lamb eternally.

Origen Adamantius (circa186–284), the first great Christian theologian, martyr, and profound student of the Bible, viewed what we have come to call hell as a place of purifying, healing, and restoring (akin to Catholicism's penitential waystation to heaven of Purgatory), not of endless sadistic torture. He taught that all creation would eventually be reconciled with God: "The doctrine of apocatastasis, commonly attributed to Origen, maintained that the entire creation, including sinners, the damned, and the devil, would finally be restored to a condition of eternal happiness and salvation. This was an important theme in early Christian eschatology."[14] It is also an important theme today, and eminent Bible scholar David Hart considers it the only one consistent with the central theme of the Bible: "If Christianity taken as a whole is indeed an entirely coherent and credible system of belief, then the universalist understanding of its message is the only one possible."[15]

Irenaeus (circa130-200) Bishop of what is now Lyons, France, is another early Church father who developed an eschatology premised on a truly omnibenevolent God and its corollary of universal salvation. Only if all souls eventually achieve salvation does the suffering of humans throughout history make sense. Following Irenaeus, theologian John Hick believes that God created the world to serve as a "vale of soul-making," or character-building. This entails "human goodness slowly built up through personal histories of moral effort has a value in the eyes of the Creator which justifies even the long travail of the soul-making process."[16] For Hick, the narrative of the soul's ascent to God is of an evolutionary journey toward perfection, beginning on Earth and continuing in the hereafter. Rather than looking backward to the fall, for which countless generations of humans bear no responsibility, Irenaean eschatology is forward-looking to future human perfection. This will be achieved by striving with faith in God and in the love of humanity in a process that extends into a postmortem existence. Universalists, therefore, believe that God's grace has no built-in time limit for us to accept or reject Him that ends at the moment of physical death. John 5:25 quite plainly affirms this: "Very truly I tell you, a time is coming and has now come when the *dead* will hear the voice of the Son of God and those who hear will live." If the dead did not get a "second chance," it would be pointless to pray for them as Paul prayed for Onesiphorous in 2 Timothy 1:16-18 (see also 1 Peter 4:6).

Gregory of Nyssa (circa 335 – 395) also believed that none of God's created creatures will fall outside His heavenly kingdom. The theme of universal salvation is seen in Gregory's words: "For it is evident that God will in truth be all in all when there shall be no evil in existence, when every created being is at harmony with itself and every tongue shall confess that Jesus Christ is Lord; when every creature shall have been made one body."[17] Traditionalists may consider the theologies of these Church fathers to be blasphemous, but Mark Scott avers that while several biblical passages imply universal salvation: "Only Matt. 25:41, 46 explicitly affirms eternal damnation, and it might reflect later theological sensibilities, not the original teachings of Jesus."[18] Jiri Moskala agrees: "Matthew 25:41, 46 does not teach eternal torment at all, despite repeated claims of the traditionalist's interpretation. The nature of the eternal punishment is not described, and it is set in contrast to eternal life, as an opposite destiny to eternal life. The eternal fire is described elsewhere in Matthew as a consuming fire, not a tormenting one."[19] Edward Fudge notes that most of the Church's founding fathers denied eternal damnation as contrary to a just and loving God: "Although not canonical, the writings of those fathers of the church are worth our reading, for these are men who were taught by the apostles, or by those whom the apostles had taught. Their writings offer a window into some of the thinking of some leaders of that early generation of believers. If we find among the apostolic fathers some unanimity of opinion, it is not to be taken for granted."[20] American Constitutional originalists make the same point when debating scholars who consider the Constitution a "living" document we can make mean anything; if you want to know what the meaning of the Constitution is, there is no better source than those who lived closest to it.

We have seen hints that no less a personage than Paul himself was a believer in universal salvation. Professor of theology Mary Getty goes further to insist that he was. She writes:

> In Romans 11, Paul develops the notion that the promise of universal salvation proceeds from God's own mercy for the enclosure of all people first in disobedience and finally in mercy or salvation. From the first chapters of the epistle, Paul has been saying that all, Jews and Gentiles alike, have sinned, rejecting God. No form of disobedience, neither Jewish nor Gentile, has limited or discouraged the salvation. ...There are two fundamental ideas that Paul cannot give up and which he tries to reconcile: that Israel is God's people and that the Gentiles have been included in the plan of God for universal salvation.[21]

Universal salvation is doubtless an appealing and spiritually satisfying doctrine, but John Sachs warns us not to take it as a blank check to do as we please because, in the end, all will be alright no matter how large one's storehouse of sins: "The gospel of God's universal saving love may not be watered down into a drug-like assurance that, regardless of what we do, 'in the end God will make everything all right,' any more than it may be distorted into the perverse announcement that God will condemn most of the world to hell"[22] Psalm 99:8 tells us that a merciful God forgives after just punishment: "LORD our God, you answered them; you were to Israel a forgiving God, though you punished their misdeeds." Clark Pinnock notes this and says: "Torturing people without end is not the sort of thing the 'Abba' Father of Jesus would do. Would God who tells us to love our enemies be intending to wreak vengeance on his enemies for all eternity?"[23] God would surely not ask us to do what He will not. Paul counsels us in Romans 12: 7 not to "repay anyone evil for evil, but take thought for what is noble in the sight of all." Again, God would not ask us to do what He will not.

Just as we may be alarmed at ordinary sinners being consigned to everlasting torment, they may also be loath to think of the truly evil—a Hitler, Stalin, or Mao—sharing eternal heavenly existence with the saintly. But according to the doctrine of conditional salvation, this will not be the ultimate fate of such evil people, for God is a just God who presumably punishes people commensurate with the evil they have done. These sadists destroyed the lives of millions and washed the 20th century in tears. Gregory, Origen, and Irenaeus taught that the truly evil will suffer the destruction of their souls in a form of spiritual capital punishment called annihilation—their souls will simply cease to be just as their earthly lives ceased to be upon corporeal death. This is the Church of England's "total non-being."

We should not worry ourselves unduly that universalism is declared heretical by some theologians and religious denominations from time to time; rather, we should be uplifted in the knowledge that God is not just a loving God, but *is* love (pure *Agape*) who will reconcile all to Himself. As the great theologian Karl Barth has said: "This much is certain, that we have no theological right to set any sort of limits to the loving kindness of God which has appeared in Jesus Christ."[24] There are some universalist theologians who refuse to set any limits on God's love, and who even reject the notion of annihilation. They see hell as a self-chosen state of punishment in the form of alienation from God; neither physical torture nor soul death. Their hell is their knowledge of eternal separation from God, and that will be the extent of their punishment. Russian theologian Sergius Bulgakov is among those universalists who followed Gregory of Nyssa, who saw hell as a condition of the soul, rather than a literal place. Bulgakov's reasoning is:

> God could not destroy his own fallen creatures, for this would indicate that he erred in creating them. On the other hand, creatures could not destroy themselves, for the power to create ex nihilo and to destroy

belonged to God alone. To admit that creaturely freedom was capable of such metaphysical suicide was to limit the power and goodness of God. He speculated that various groups of people would participate in the general resurrection differently: "the saintly figures would do so actively and willingly, while the indifferent and the wicked souls would accept the resurrection as inevitable."[25]

Why the Debate?

Richard Harries asks: "So how did it all go so wrong? The great St Augustine of Hippo is the culprit here, leading the whole Western tradition astray, giving rulers and churchmen alike the tools to terrify people into good behaviour."[26] But let's not put all the blame on Augustine. Although his view has been the orthodox view for centuries, Harold Booher writes: "Clark Pinnock urges: 'although there are many good reasons for questioning the orthodox view of the nature of hell, the most important reason is the fact that the Bible does not teach it. ... it is a little annoying to be told that no biblical case can be made for annihilation of the wicked when it is the traditional view that most needs proving.'"[27]

If, as Pinnock says, hell is unbiblical, why is the concept so prevalent? Part of the problem is that it suited the Church and the secular authorities to terrorize simple-minded peasants into behaving themselves, but the problem lies mostly in translations. The words *Sheol*, *Hades*, and *Gehenna* account for nearly all the translations into hell in the Old and New Testaments. The Hebrew word *Sheol* and the Greek word *Hades* always referred to the grave or the state of death in the Old Testament, yet in the King James Bible, they are translated from Latin as hell (some have called this the "Latin heresy"). Significantly, the original Hebrew and Greek meanings are retained in modern versions of the Bible. Aaron Milavec observes that: "Hades was the mythical abode of the dead—a borrowing from Hellenistic culture—and should be understood as quite distinct from what the medievalists later identified as 'hell.' The original intent of 'he was not abandoned to Hades' in a sermon in Acts (2:31) was to reinforce the reality of the death of Jesus prior to his resurrection."[28]

Yet another, more problematic, word traditionally translated as hell is *Gehenna*. *Gehenna* is a Greek transliteration from the Hebrew "Valley of Hinnom," and is a literal place in old Jerusalem that contained a continually burning garbage dump with a sordid history of idolatry, cruelty, and injustice. It was here that child sacrifices were offered to the pagan god Molech, and where "unclean" bodies and slain enemies were cast. The fires of Gehenna later became a metaphor for hell. Jesus used the word *Gehenna* more than anyone else in Scripture, but biblical scholars have different views as to the meaning He had in mind. One of them, Rodney Duke, notes that: "Hades and Gehenna have popularly, but wrongly, been conflated into a composite image of 'hell.'" He also informs us that in Jesus' time: "Jewish and Christian audiences recognized Gehenna as a final judgment image of a place where bodies would be left to decay unburied," and that the poetic "language of everlasting worms, smoke, fire, punishment, destruction, etc. communicated the lasting result rather than a never-ending process."[29]

Hell, or universal salvation? The great theologian, N. T. Wright, says that God's love wins:

> When Jesus was warning his hearers about Gehenna he was not, as a general rule, telling them that unless they repented in this life they would burn in the next one. As with God's kingdom, so with its opposite: it is on earth that things matter, not somewhere else. His message to His contemporaries was stark... Unless they turned back from their hopeless and rebellious dreams of establishing God's kingdom in their own terms... Rome would turn Jerusalem into a hideous, stinking extension of its own smoldering rubbish heap. When Jesus said "Unless you repent, you will all likewise perish," that is the primary meaning He had in mind.[30]

Wright continues: "The New Testament, true to its Old Testament roots, regularly insists that the major, central concern is God's purpose of rescue and re-creation for the whole world, the entire cosmos." [31]

Although I am very far from being a biblical scholar, as I see it, one's views on hell arise from different understandings of God. Traditionalists imply that God's love is ultimately limited to those who accept Him, and He demonstrates His justice by eternally punishing those who have not accepted His offer of salvation while alive. Universalists believe that God's love is unconditional, pure *Agape*. He could not possibly condemn His creatures to eternal torture because of their ignorance but demonstrates his justice by ultimately saving all by purifying them and providing a new chance for them to accept Him postmortem, but annihilates the truly evil and the unrepentant and creates everything anew.

In the final analysis, we have to say that it's a mystery and we just don't know. We should all humbly admit that St. Augustine, despite his dogmatic insistence on a literal hell, had the right attitude about the interpretation of Holy Scripture:

> In matters that are obscure and far beyond our vision, even in such as we may find treated in Holy Scripture, different Interpretations are sometimes possible without prejudice to the faith we have received. In

such a case, we should not rush in headlong and so firmly take our stand on one side that, if further progress in the search of truth justly undermines this position, we too fall with it. That would be to battle not for the teaching of Holy Scripture but for our own, wishing its teaching to conform to ours, whereas we ought to wish ours to conform to that of Sacred Scripture.[32]

And as Deuteronomy 29:29 informs us: "The secret things belong to the LORD our God, but the things revealed belong to us and to our children forever, that we may follow all the words of this law." This is telling us that eschatological matters are the secret matters of God we are not meant to know. But my personal belief is that eternal torture is wildly inconsistent with any logical understanding of God's love, mercy, and justice, and with His promise of final victory over evil. Christians can politely differ on this issue, as many have in all denominations from the earliest times, and remain within the bounds of orthodoxy. We need not adhere to either position in the way we adhere to the foundational dogmas of the Trinity, the Incarnation, and the bodily resurrection of Christ.

It is worth noting that even Catholicism, which long followed Augustine's view of hell, is having second thoughts. As Pope John Paul II noted: "The images of hell that Sacred Scripture presents to us must be correctly interpreted. They show the complete frustration and emptiness of life without God. Rather than a place, hell indicates a state of those who freely and definitively separate themselves from God, the source of all life and joy." [33] This is almost identical to Bulgakov's reasoning noted earlier, as well as with most of the early church fathers.

Notes

1. MacDonald, H., 1985, pp. 38-40.
2. In Gerstner, J., 1980, p. 53.
3. Talbot, T., 1990, p. 22.
4. Sachs, J., 1991, p. 231.
5. Jordan, J., 2012, p. 53.
6. Hick, J., 1998, p. 26.
7. Church of England's Doctrine Commission, 1995, p. 199.
8. Bray, G. 1992, p. 23.
9. In Lane, A. 1981, p. 74.
10. Boettner, L., 2017, p. 30.
11. In Lane, A., 1981, p. 74.
12. Sachs, J., 1991, p. 227.
13. Sachs, J., 1991, p. 228.
14. Harries, R., 2020, p.13.
15. Hart, D., 2019, p. 3.

16. Hick, J., 2007, p. 256.
17. In Pearson, C., 2009, p. 28.
18. Scott, M., 2010 p. 321.
19. Moskala, J. 2015, p. 115.
20. Fudge, E., 2012, p. 353.
21. Getty, M., 1988, p. 463 and p. 468.
22. Sachs, J., 1991, p. 234.
23. Pinnock, C., 1992, p. 140.
24. Barth, K., 1960, pp. 61-62.
25. In Gavrilyuk, P., 2006. p.118.
26. Harries, R., 2020, p. 14.
27. Booher, H., 2013, np.
28. Milavec, A., 2021, p. 1.
29. Duke, R., 2017, p. 255.
30. Wright, N., 2008, p. 176
31. Wright, N., 2008, p. 184.
32. In Collins, F., 2006, p. 83.
33. In Horn, T., 2017, pp. 197-198.

Chapter 5

The Resurrection:
The Event that Changed Everything

The Bedrock of Christianity

Two thousand years ago an explosive event took place that reframed all subsequent human history—the death and Resurrection of Jesus Christ. The Resurrection was no "ordinary" miracle (if we can conceive of any miracle this way) because it signified the end of the old covenant and the birth of the new—the New Creation. Other biblical miracles resolved earthly issues for specific individuals or groups of individuals, such as the parting of the waters, healing the afflicted, or feeding the five thousand, whereas the Resurrection miracle applies to all God's creatures and is the unfolding of biblical eschatology. No other event in the history of mankind has had such an impact on the lives of so many people around the world. Jesus' Resurrection on Easter Sunday, predicted in the Old Testament by Christ Himself, was an affirmation of His identity as the Son of God and of the Atonement, redemption, reconciliation, and salvation. It is a miraculous event that many people just cannot believe, and even practicing Christians find it difficult to comprehend and defend it. Nevertheless, it is indisputable that the Resurrection of Christ is the bedrock of Christianity because without it there is no Christianity. Paul himself said as much in Corinthians 15:14-17:

> And if Christ has not been raised, our preaching is useless and so is your faith. More than that, we are then found to be false witnesses about God, for we have testified about God that he raised Christ from the dead. But he did not raise him if in fact the dead are not raised. For if the dead are not raised, then Christ has not been raised either. And if Christ has not been raised, your faith is futile; you are still in your sins.

In Corinthians verses 20-22, Paul emphatically tells us that Jesus did rise from the dead because he was a personal witness to it. But we didn't witness the risen Christ, so why should we believe in the Resurrection? Millions of people in the ancient world did not witness the event either, and we assume that they would be just as skeptical and dismissive as you or I about a story of a dead man rising to life from the grave. There must have been something very special about the event and its message because it spread quickly, and with unreasonable success, across the ancient Roman world. Unlike the spread of Islam by the sword, Christianity spread by the power of persuasion alone. It lacked any political or military power, indeed, it prevailed against the violent military power of Rome, as well as against the considerable authoritative power of the Jewish leaders to quash it. It all started with a small group of impoverished and disempowered Jews in Jerusalem and quickly spread to Jews and gentiles alike throughout the Roman Empire and then around the world.

Because the Resurrection is at the heart of Christianity, it has been scrutinized like no other event in history. The Resurrection is a weighty scholarly enterprise. Typing "Resurrection of Jesus" into the Google Scholar search engine spits out 265,000 articles and books, so there is vastly more to be said than I can say here. Among the many books on the subject, N.T. Wright's *The Resurrection of the Son of God* runs 817 pages, and William Lane Craig's *The Historical Argument for the Resurrection of Jesus* contains 678 pages. In these thousands of books and articles, authors from every academic discipline and belief system have weighed in to debate everything related to it. They even argue over the meaning of a single noun or verb written in Greek, Hebrew, or Aramaic. Andrew Loke wrote a large book (*Investigating the resurrection of Jesus Christ: a new transdisciplinary approach*) detailing, evaluating, and apparently reconciling these minor squabbles over seeming contradictions or emphases in the Resurrection narratives in scripture that are of interest only to professional theologians. We are not getting into depths where we may get lost; rather we concentrate on the Resurrection event itself, the historical evidence for it, and the naturalistic accounts that attempt to deny it.

The Nature of Historical Explanation

Examine virtually any non-trivial event that theists, atheists, and agnostics alike agree occurred and you will find that they most probably disagree on how to interpret it. This is especially true of the Resurrection. Christians see it as a miraculous act of God, but atheists and agnostics will either reject it or look for some naturalistic explanation. Note the initial strong disagreement over the beginning of the universe, the "inaugural" miracle, since even the coming of Jesus and his Resurrection depended on the existence of a universe in which those things occurred. Theists say that God created it, atheists, if reluctantly pushed into explaining how we got something from nothing, will say it created itself. In other words, both acknowledge that the universe exists but differ radically on how to account for it. Facts of great meaning rarely speak the same language to everyone, and thus we tend to interpret them from our philosophical mother tongues.

The Resurrection

Given a variety of explanations for an observed phenomenon, science opts for the one with the greatest power, scope, and predictive power. That is, it opts for the explanation that best coheres with all the facts at hand with the fewest assumptions; accounts for more of those facts than alternative explanations, and provides hypotheses guiding the search for additional facts. Facts are like pieces of a jigsaw puzzle; they don't mean much in isolation. Facts, like jigsaw pieces, must slot in nicely and add meaning to the big picture. I do not mean to suggest that we accept or reject the Resurrection based on science. I accept it on the basis of eyewitness accounts, and biblical interpretation of those accounts in the same way that I accept that a battle occurred at Gettysburg in 1863. We should examine the evidence on its merits and neither accept nor reject it by appealing to *a priori* presuppositions.

Christianity's interpretation of the recorded facts of Easter Sunday is not accepted by atheists, and Richard Lewontin tells us why. He says that while scientists are not compelled by science to opt only for naturalistic/materialistic explanations; rather, it is their *a priori* commitment to them that compels them: "Moreover, that materialism is absolute, for we cannot allow a Divine Foot in the door."[1] In other words, if scientists affirm that the natural and the material is all there is, they will reject any miraculous interpretation of events, not because the evidence is weak, but because it does not match the furniture in their minds. There are many scientists of great stature who in their daily grind work within a naturalistic/materialist framework while denying that it is the only way of knowing, and who do affirm the Resurrection as a historical fact.

Explaining historical events to everyone's satisfaction is inherently more difficult than explaining scientific observations. History concerns itself with the particular or the unique in messy human affairs rather than with generalizations about the predicable natural world. The Resurrection of Christ is by definition a non-repeatable phenomenon, so it has no predictive power (unless we count a prediction an Apostle may have made that it would lead to the explosive rise of Christianity). Every specific event in history is non-repeatable: Constantine with never cross the Rubicon again, Hitler will never hold another Nuremberg rally, and science will never see another Big Bang. Historians do not observe events as they take place. Rather, they consult original documents, the credibility and number of witnesses attesting to them, and archeological findings. These data are analyzed and synthesized in an attempt to link historical events to one another and provide an explanation as to why events unfolded the way they did. These data are subjected to what historians call "source criticism," and are accepted or rejected based on general consensus.

After scrutinizing all data regarding an event, just like scientists, historians then reason to the best explanation. If all available data converge to agree to the event's actual occurrence, historians consider it proven "beyond a reasonable doubt." As C. Behan McCullagh describes this process: "if the scope and strength of an explanation are very great, so that it explains a large number and variety of facts, many more than any competing explanation, then it is likely to be true."[2] Thus, like scientific explanations, an historical explanation is considered likely true to the extent that it gathers more facts under its umbrella (its scope) and has the ability to effectively explain the matter in question without the need for further suppositions (its power) than competing explanations. Unlike finding a consensus among scientists, arriving at a consensus about historical matters may take many decades or even centuries.

The Minimal Facts of the Resurrection

Gary Habermas outlines a "minimal facts" approach to Jesus' death and Resurrection that is agreed upon by virtually all scholars of the event. These minimal facts are: "(1) Jesus died due to the process of crucifixion. (2) Very soon afterwards, Jesus' disciples had experiences that they believed were appearances of the resurrected Jesus. (3) Just a few years later, Saul of Tarsus also experienced what he thought was a post-Resurrection appearance of the risen Jesus."[3] As the number of events relating to the Resurrection rise beyond these three facts, the level of agreement sinks. However, the majority of critical scholars view the conversion of James, Jesus' earthly skeptical brother, as one of the major proofs of the Resurrection, and between two-thirds and three-quarters of the scholars "favor the tomb being empty for other than natural reasons [e.g., Jesus' body was stolen]."[4] Thus, the majority of scholars who have seriously studied the evidence agree on these five foundational facts.

The Resurrection of Christ has been shown time and again to be a better explanation for each of these core facts than any other, both individually and as a coherent whole. That is, it has greater explanatory scope and greater explanatory power than alternative explanations. Any naturalistic alternative theory has to explain away all the agreed-upon facts, to at least present a plausible alternative to them, and explain other historical facts, such as the conversions of James and Paul and the rapid growth of Christianity. But all naturalistic explanations collapse under their own meager weight once they are examined. If the Resurrection did not occur, it is strange that no alternative explanation of the agreed-upon facts has ever emerged to the level of even minimal consensus. What is more, each naturalist account claims only to explain a single fact, such as why the tomb was empty or what it was the apostles claimed to have witnessed. The Resurrection claim, however, explains all the known facts coherently.

It is not only Christian scholars who have come to affirm the Resurrection as factual. Pinchas Lapide, a Jewish theologian and Israeli historian, wrote a book-length defense of the Resurrection. As noted in Chapter One, God maintains an epistemic distance from us and cannot be proven with absolute scientific certainty. Likewise: "Lapide emphasizes throughout that the Resurrection, like any experience of God, can be grasped only by faith. It can never be proved conclusively. The reason is summed up pithily in the words of Edward Schweizer when he speaks of God 'renouncing anything that would compel men to believe.' Or as Karl Jaspers puts it, 'a proven God is no God.'"[5] Lapide is, of course, quite correct: the Christian explanation of the Resurrection cannot be conclusively proven, but it can be proven by the "beyond a reasonable doubt" criterion demanded by the Anglo-American common law system.

Craig Keener is one of the World's leading Biblical scholars who was formerly an atheist but was led to Christ by his studies of the Resurrection. He said in an interview with Sean McDowell: "The Lord keeps renewing my strength. I can't forget what he's done for me–how he converted me from atheism by a direct and utterly unmerited encounter with his Spirit in the gospel. Even when I was an atheist, I said that if I discovered that there really was a God, I would give him everything, because I would owe him everything."[6] Then we have Rudolf Bultmann, a renowned skeptic of the New Testament, writing: "The Christian fellowship was convinced that Jesus had done miracles and they told many stories of miracles about him… But there can be no doubt that Jesus did such deeds, which were, in his and his contemporaries' understanding, miracles; that is to say, events that were the result of supernatural divine causality. Doubtless he healed the sick and cast out demons."[7]

The Resurrection and Miracles

Regardless of the weight of the historical evidence supporting the truth of the Resurrection, the greatest barrier to belief is that the Resurrection of the dead defies Hume's "normal course of events." By definition, miracles are abnormal and non-reproducible, so they cannot be proved or disproved by science. But science is not the only way of knowing, and the historical evidence for the Resurrection is as good as, or better than, the evidence for almost any event in ancient history. Steven Davis notes that believers in the Resurrection stress the unity of agreement among the authors of the New Testament that Jesus rose from the dead, and certain facts surrounding the Resurrection are not denied by competent historical scholarship. He also notes the inability of any viable naturalistic explanation for the facts and concludes: "The most plausible explanation of these facts—so believers in the Resurrection will argue—is that Jesus did indeed rise from the dead and show himself to the disciples. It does not seem sensible to claim that the Christian Church, a spiritual movement whose vitality changed the world, was started by charlatans or dupes."[8] Despite his endorsement of the Resurrection, Davis then plays devil's advocate to give rational reasons for non-believers to doubt it: "What are the chances that a man dead for three days would live again? In short, the non-believer will claim that even if the believer's arguments are strong and even if non-believers can't say for sure what did happen, by far the most sensible position is to deny that the resurrection occurred."[9]

Davis also says that even if the probability that the Resurrection occurred is 99%, its occurrence still has to be rejected from a naturalist point of view, because in the realm of human experience, dead men do not naturally rise from the grave, and I agree 100%; dead people don't "naturally" rise from the grave. But Davis's conclusion from this perspective (not his personal conclusion, for he believed in the Resurrection) is already decided by deduction from the self-evident premise that dead men don't naturally rise again. Davis is basically saying if non-believers admit the historicity of the Resurrection, they would be admitting that miracles occur, and because miracles are said to violate the laws of nature and our uniform experience of those laws, they must be ruled out *a priori*. If miracles are ruled out *a priori*, how do those non-believers who admit the minimalist facts of the Resurrection account for those facts? That is the topic of the next chapter; for now, we look at the evidence from the New Testament and from archaeology.

Evidence from the New Testament

The primary evidence of the Resurrection comes from the New Testament. An atheist will object to this and might say: "Okay, the Resurrection hypothesis may have greater explanatory scope and power than other hypotheses, and that all alternative hypotheses accept the Gospel accounts that '*something*' happened to change human history. But how do we know that we can trust the New Testament accounts?" One very strong reason is the exponential growth of the Church very shortly after the written documents were distributed, but how do we know that the original accounts have been accurately transmitted? During the nineteenth- and early twentieth centuries, the focus seemed to be heavily weighted by scholarly intentions to prove the Bible to be inaccurate. One such scholar was Sir William Ramsay, a major scholar of Middle Eastern history. Ramsay intensively researched the New Testament book of Acts and the Gospel of Luke for decades with such an intent. However, his studies of the historicity of these books led him to change his mind and his heart and became a Christian, writing: "I take the view that Luke's history is unsurpassed in regard to its trustworthiness . . . You may press the words of Luke in a degree beyond any other historian's, and they stand the keenest scrutiny and the hardest treatment, provided always that the critic knows the subject and does not go beyond the limits of science and of justice."[10]

Historians and biblical scholars examine the reliability of the transmission of documents from the ancient world in two ways. First, they look at the number of existing copies of the original text, and second, they look at the time gap between the earliest existing manuscripts and the time when the original was written. A text is considered reliable to the extent that the number of existing manuscripts is large and the time gap between them and the event they portray is short. The more original manuscripts there are, and the shorter the time gap between the historical event in question and its documentation, the better they are able to reconstruct and assess the veracity of the original manuscript.

As for the time gap criterion, William Albright, regarded as the father of modern archaeology, notes that: "We can already say emphatically that there is no longer any solid basis for dating any book of the New Testament after about A.D. 80, two full generations before the date of between A.D. 130 and 150 given by the more radical New Testament critics of today."[11] Sir Frederick Kenyon, an expert in ancient texts and former director of the British Museum, writes: "The interval then between the dates of original composition and the earliest extant evidence becomes so small as to be in fact negligible, and the last foundation for any doubt that the Scriptures have come down to us substantially as they were written has now been removed. Both the authenticity and the general integrity of the books of the New Testament may be regarded as finally established."[12] By way of contrast, the time gap for the earliest existing manuscripts of the average ancient author is about 500 years after the events depicted.

Documentation of the scriptures of other religions pales in comparison to the documentation of the Christian scriptures. Mohammad's biography was not written until 135 years after his death; the first biography of Buddha was written 700 years after his death, and the scriptures of Zoroastrianism were not committed to writing for about 1,300 years after Zoroaster died.[13] The New Testament books were written almost as an ancient equivalent of a modern "news flash" by eyewitnesses to the events they document; no other ancient document can claim that. The New Testament was written when many of Christ's Roman and Jewish enemies were still living, which would have prompted their authors to be very careful about the truth of their statements. Any errors appearing in their accounts would have certainly been exposed.

In terms of the number of existing manuscripts, the New Testament wins hands down over any other ancient texts. Porter and Pitts note: "When compared with other works of antiquity, the New Testament has far greater (numerical) and earlier documentation than any other book. Most of the available works of antiquity have only a few manuscripts that attest to their existence, and these are typically much later than their original date of composition, so that it is not uncommon for the earliest manuscript to be dated over nine hundred years after the original composition."[14] The works of Plato have 210 manuscripts, with the earliest copy dated at 900AD, or 1,200 years after the events. Aristotle's work has 1,000 manuscripts also dated 1,200 years after the events. Herodotus' work has 109 manuscripts, with the earliest copy dated 1,350 years after the events, and Thucydides' work has 50 manuscripts with the earliest dated 1,300 years after the events. Homer's *Iliad* is second to the New Testament in number and time gap with 1,757 manuscripts, with the earliest dated 400 years after the recorded events. By way of contrast, McDowell and Casey document 21,362 New Testament Greek manuscripts dated between 50 and 100AD, or about 15 to 85 years after the recorded events. This comparative documentation led Frederick Kenyon to remark: "The number of manuscripts of the New Testament, of early translations from it, and of quotations from it in the oldest writers of the Church, is so large that it is practically certain that the true reading of every doubtful passage is preserved in some one or other of these ancient authorities. This can be said of no other ancient book in the world."[15]

As Steven Cowan remarks about the Bible:

> The texts of the Old and New Testaments have been remarkably preserved through thousands of years of copying; the historical assertions of both Testaments have been seen to be reliable; the ethical teachings and assumptions of Scripture are rationally defensible when rightly interpreted; the Bible's teachings are consistent with the best contemporary science; and the canonization process faithfully delivered to the church a collection of new covenant documents that bear the apostolic imprimatur. What's more, there are no proven contradictions in the Bible regarding either its historical or theological teachings. The Bible presents a consistent, unified message concerning the great drama of God's redemption of fallen humanity through the life, death, and resurrection of Jesus Christ.[16]

Thus, according to universally accepted criteria for judging the trustworthiness of ancient documents, the New Testament has been accurately transmitted. Historians consider other ancient documents accurately transmitted whose manuscripts are far fewer and far between the date when the earliest existing copy was penned. If skeptics reject the transmitted reliability of the New Testament, according to their own criteria of reliability they must reject all other manuscripts of antiquity because they fail miserably in comparison with the New Testament. There cannot be one standard for secular documents and another for religious documents if the game is to be fair. New Testament scholar

F.F. Bruce notes the anti-Christian bias and double standard among biblical critics when he writes: "The evidence for our New Testament writings is ever so much greater than the evidence for many writings of classical authors, the authenticity of which no one dreams of questioning. And if the New Testament were a collection of secular writings, the authenticity would generally be regarded as beyond all doubt."[17]

The Bible and the Archaeological Record

The science of archaeology, while adding greatly to our understanding of the ancient world, cannot be said to "prove" the Bible. Scientists don't like the word "prove;" they prefer "provides evidence for." As if to vindicate Psalm 85:11: "Truth shall spring out of the earth," archaeology has done that in spades. The Bible contains a number of names of places and people previously thought not found elsewhere, which moved critics in the past to dismiss the Bible. Then along came the discipline of archaeology in the nineteenth century to upset the skeptics' applecart by providing independent evidence that those people and places existed. For instance, there is no mention of Jesus' childhood home of Nazareth existing in the first century AD in any surviving historical literature outside the Bible. This led some critics to argue that its existence in the time of Jesus was a religious hoax. Then in 2009, archaeologists unearthed a house from first-century Nazareth.[18] There have been numerous archaeological discoveries corroborating biblical claims, and none that have contradicted them. A 2014 article in the *Biblical Archaeology Review* noted that at least 50 people in the Bible previously thought to be fictitious have been confirmed by archaeological discoveries to be real people.[19]

Archaeology has thus been an ally of Christianity for 175 years by yanking various biblical places and personages out of the realm of myth into the realm of history. Eric Metaxas notes that the first archaeological find that corroborated the Bible occurred in 1846 when an Assyrian obelisk was discovered referring to Jehu, a ninth-century BC Hebrew king, and that: "This trend of archaeology corroborating Biblical accounts continued so consistently that in 1959 Rabbi Dr. Nelson Glueck declared 'no archaeological discovery has ever controverted a biblical reference.' Since then, the evidence has kept coming."[20] Another scholar noted the value of archaeology to the Bible: "Less than a century ago, the agnostic took great glee in sneeringly referring to the 'hundreds of historical mistakes' in the Bible. But then came the science of archaeology, and with each shovelful of dirt the sneers have become less visible, until today they scarcely can be seen."[21] And yet another who, after recognizing how naysayers seized upon apparent conflicts in detail between archaeological data and biblical history, concludes: "Nevertheless, every generation of negative critics will find itself in perpetual strategic retreat, as advancing archaeology relentlessly contradicts the examples of alleged Biblical error most confidently publicized by their fathers."[22]

Archaeology cannot tell us anything about the Resurrection itself since it left no archaeological record to be dug up; its value lies in confirming the book that does. Although the Bible is a collection of 66 books (or 73 books in Catholicism) written by more than 40 authors over a period of more than 1,500 years, it is amazingly accurate when it comes to the historical record. Independent documentary evidence of the Bible was found in 1947 by young Bedouins tending their goats and sheep near Qumran, close to the Dead Sea. They discovered a collection of large clay jars in a cave, several of which contained papyrus scrolls that have come to be called the Dead Sea scrolls. When word of this got out, scores of archaeologists and treasure hunters combed nearby caves and unearthed thousands of fragments that made up between 800 and 900 manuscripts dating from the third century BC. to the first century AD. The Dead Sea Scrolls (actually, mostly fragments that had to be laboriously reconstructed over decades) contain every book of the Old Testament except the Book of Esther. Eugene Ulrich notes that:

> Among the first discoveries in 1947 were two scrolls of the Book of Isaiah. One large but fragmentary scroll (lQIsab) appeared to agree almost word for word with the traditional Hebrew text, the Masoretic (MT). This scroll, published quickly by 1954, served to support the confidence of scholars that our traditional texts had maintained an amazing accuracy throughout the centuries of repeated hand copying until the invention of the printing press.[23]

Millar Burrows notes about the Isaiah scroll: "Of the 166 *words* in Isaiah 53, there are only seventeen *letters* in question. Ten of these letters are simply a matter of spelling, which does not affect the sense. Four more letters are minor stylistic changes, such as conjunctions. The remaining three letters comprise the word 'light,' which is added in verse 11, and does not affect the meaning greatly."[24] Thus, we can trust the biblical account of the Resurrection because we can trust the Bible.

Notes

1. Lewontin, R., 1977, np.
2. McCullagh, C., 1984, p. 26.
3. Habermas, G., 2012, p. 21.
4. Ibid., p. 22.
5. In Kennedy, K., 1985, p.441.
6. In McDowell, S. 2019, np.
7. In Crenshaw, S., 2009, p. 75.

8. Davis, S., 1984, pp. 152-153.
9. Ibid, p. 154.
10. Ramsay, W., 1975, p. 89.
11. Albright, W., 1955, p. 136.
12. In McRoberts, K., 2011, p. 97.
13. Strobel, L. 1998, p. 87 (quoting ancient historian Edwin Yamauchi).
14. Porter, S. & Pitts, A., 2015, p. 50.
15. In Berkhof, L., 1996, p. 159.
16. Cowan, S., 2013, p. 461.
17. In Brown, M., 2006, p. 43.
18. Alexandre, Y., 2020.
19. Mykytiuk, L., 2014.
20. Metaxas, E., 2021, np.
21. Willmington, H., 2019, p.1.
22. Kline, M., 1963, p. 151.
23. Ulrich, E., 2004, p. 2.
24. Burrows, M., 1986, p. 304.

Chapter 6

Secular Attempts to Explain the Resurrection

The Stolen Body Theory

There are a number of secular hypotheses relating to the Resurrection of Jesus, none of which, even if we entertain the notion that they may be right, purport to explain more than one of the minimal facts surrounding the Resurrection. All hypotheses offered as alternatives to the biblical account are premised on the "impossibility of miracles." Most of them were discredited soon after they were posited in the scholarly community, but we still see them bandied about on atheist websites and occasionally in the scholarly literature. This is why Christians should be aware of them. We begin with the empty tomb discovered by Mary Magdalene on the Sunday following Jesus' death on the cross. The reason there is near unanimity among scholars of all worldviews that the tomb was empty is that the Jewish authorities did not deny it. When the Roman guards informed members of the Sanhedrin (the Jewish high courts that had condemned Jesus and asked Pontius Pilate to crucify Him) of the empty tomb they attempted to explain it away by claiming that the disciples had stolen the body. As Matthew 28: 11-15 tells it:

> While the women were on their way, some of the guards went into the city and reported to the chief priests everything that had happened. When the chief priests had met with the elders and devised a plan, they gave the soldiers a large sum of money, telling them, "You are to say, 'His disciples came during the night and stole him away while we were asleep.' If this report gets to the governor, we will satisfy him and keep you out of trouble." So the soldiers took the money and did as they were instructed. And this story has been widely circulated among the Jews to this very day.

Indeed, a letter circulating in the Jewish community was recorded by Justin Martyr in his *Dialogue with Trypho* (a Jewish rabbi) in about 165 AD which read: "[A] godless and lawless heresy had sprung from one Jesus, a Galilean deceiver, whom we crucified, but his disciples stole him by night from the tomb, where he was laid when unfastened from the cross, and now deceive men by asserting that he has risen from the dead and ascended to heaven."[1]

The Jewish response to the empty tomb is itself proof from a hostile source that the tomb was indeed empty. If the tomb had not been empty, it would have been easy for the Jewish leadership to retrieve the body and parade it around Jerusalem, thus squelching the nascent Christian movement for all time. After all, having witnessed the risen Christ, it was in that very city that the apostles began preaching the message. If the tomb had not been empty, the apostles' Resurrection proclamation could not be maintained for a single hour. William Lane Craig adds to this the evidence of the rapid appearance of the Gospels in Jerusalem:

> The Gospels were written in such a temporal and geographical proximity to the events they record that it would have been almost impossible to fabricate events.... The fact that the disciples were able to proclaim the Resurrection in Jerusalem in the face of their enemies a few weeks after the crucifixion shows that what they proclaimed was true, for they could never have proclaimed the Resurrection (and been believed) under such circumstances had it not occurred.[2]

The notion that the disciples stole Jesus' body cannot tell us how or why the disciples in their hour of despair, confusion, and doubt would get around the Roman guards to steal the body. Certainly, a frightened rabble of fishermen and reviled tax collectors were no match for trained and well-armed Roman legionnaires. If the guards were asleep (a very serious charge for a Roman soldier), how could the disciples have rolled away the massive stone sealing the tomb and taken Jesus' body without waking them? Recall that the guards identified the disciples as the thieves, so why was there no evidence of a struggle with them? Most tellingly, why would the guards have to explain anything at all if the tomb was not empty? If the authorities had any evidence that the disciples had stolen the body, why were they not arrested immediately and placed on trial?

What would be the disciples' motive for stealing the body anyway? The possession of a dead and decaying body would could not possibly be something that would transform the followers of Jesus from the fearful cowards they admitted they were to fearless champions of His message.

Why would they risk their lives for such a fiction? Andrew Loke notes that: "these disciples knew that their leader (i.e., Jesus) was already vilified and brutally crucified, and yet they chose to proclaim him knowing that a similar fate could well befall them for doing that. After all, it was usual to execute the followers of insurgents alongside them, and it is likely that most of the followers of Jesus were hiding, in fear of their lives, at the time of his death"[3]

After Jesus' ignominious death, His dispirited and frightened followers scattered lest they be subjected to the same fate. They could have gone back to their normal lives, thankful to have escaped from Jerusalem with their lives, and returned to Torah-based religious observance. They clearly did not do that; instead, they went about the Jewish and pagan lands preaching that the risen Jesus was the Messiah. The disciples firmly believed in the risen Christ for they had seen him, as did many others. The transformation of the lives of the disciples from a group of disheartened men (recall that even Peter denied Christ three times), the fact that they risked their lives on their conviction, and the fact that the authorities could have easily falsified their claim if it was false, thoroughly discredits the conspiracy hypothesis.

The Wrong Tomb Theory

The wrong tomb theory maintains that when the women returned to the tomb on Easter Sunday they simply went to the wrong tomb and found it empty. That's the end of its explanatory scope; *everyone* forgot where Jesus was buried. Ron Rhodes remarks about this collective amnesia: "To believe in this theory, we'd have to conclude that the women went to the wrong tomb, that Peter and John ran to the wrong tomb, that the Jews then went to the wrong tomb, followed by the Jewish Sanhedrin and the Romans, who also went to the wrong tomb. We'd also have to say that Joseph of Arimathea, the owner of the tomb, also went to the wrong tomb. We'd even have to say the angel from heaven appeared at the wrong tomb."[4] And Gary Gromacki notes:

> The gospels of Matthew, Mark, and John specifically mention that Mary Magdalene went to the tomb of Jesus early in the morning and she was present when Joseph of Arimathea and Nicodemus buried the body of Jesus. If the women went to the wrong tomb, then the Jews or Romans could have gone to the right tomb and produced the body of Jesus and that would have stopped the story that Jesus had risen from the dead. The fact that the Jews bribed the Roman guards to say that the disciples of Jesus stole his body while they slept at night is evidence of the fact that they could not produce the body of Jesus because it was gone.[5]

Let us also not forget that the Jewish and Roman authorities knew the location of the tomb, and posted guards there and that Peter and John found it, thus confirming the women correctly indicated its location. How would finding an empty tomb convince the disciples that Jesus had risen from the dead without the additional evidence of His many appearances anyway? An empty tomb without a risen Christ would be as empty of meaning as this theory.

The Fraud or Conspiracy Theory

The fraud theory argues that Jesus conspired with various others, such as Joseph of Arimathea, to convince the disciples that He was the Messiah by manipulating matters to make it appear that He was the fulfillment of Old Testament prophecies. However, it all backfired when the drugs Jesus allegedly took to revive Him could not fight his horrific wounds and he died. The conspirators then stole the body and disposed of it. Regarding his many appearances, the theory maintains that it was a case of mistaken identity. Some versions of this theory even maintain that Jesus has a twin brother and that it was His twin who appeared to the disciples and in public. Other versions argue that the apostles were a party to the fraud from the beginning, but Blaise Pascal observes:

> The hypothesis that the Apostles were knaves is quite absurd. Follow it out to the end, and imagine these twelve men meeting after Jesus' death and conspiring to say that he had risen from the dead. This means attacking all the powers that be. The human heart is singularly susceptible to fickleness, to change, to promises, to bribery. One of them had only to deny his story under these inducements, or still more because of possible imprisonment, tortures and death, and they would all have been lost. Follow that out.[6]

The theory paints Jesus Christ Himself as a knave by deceitfully seeking to convince people of His messiahship. But Jesus lived his earthy life as the highest of moral characters, consistently and forcefully condemning lying and deceitful behavior. To think that Jesus would preach and live such a saintly life while inwardly seeking some kind of worldly advantage stretches credulity to the breaking point. Surely in the face of social ostracism and death, the apostles would have asked themselves: "'Why are we continuing to tell this lie together anyway?' Moreover, lying about such a fundamental matter concerning their faith would be inconsistent with their devotion to the God of Israel. For according to their beliefs, to make up Jesus' resurrection would be judged guilty as false witnesses and condemned by the God of Israel."[7]

The Swoon Theory

Another theory of the empty tomb is that Jesus had not died on the cross, but rather He passed out ("swooned") and was resuscitated in the tomb. This incredible swoon theory assumes that a man who suffered the grotesque torture of a skin-tearing flogging, six-inch spikes driven into His hands and feet, hung on a cross until He could no longer pull Himself up to breathe, and had a spear thrust into His side from which "blood and water" flowed, could be resuscitated. His Roman executioners knew that He died because they did not break His legs, which was the usual culmination of crucifixion. His executioners would have faced death themselves if they had not made certain Jesus was dead. After being laid in His tomb, Jesus was embalmed in spice and wrapped in a weighty shroud. A still-living man would not survive such treatment. If He did survive, how would He have been able to roll the huge stone, weighing as much as 2,000 pounds, away and then escape the Roman guards? Further, when he appeared to the disciples, it was not as a bloody mess, but rather as a wholesome body with clean wounds that he invited them to inspect. It was medically impossible for Jesus to have survived His ordeal. As a detailed and gruesomely illustrated article in the *Journal of the American Medical Association* put it:

> Clearly, the weight of historical and medical evidence indicates that Jesus was dead before the wound to his side was inflicted and supports the traditional view that the spear, thrust between his right ribs, probably perforated not only the right lung but also the pericardium and heart and thereby ensured his death. Accordingly, interpretations based on the assumption that Jesus did not die on the cross appear to be at odds with modern medical knowledge.[8]

The Legend Theory

According to the legend theory (a variation of the fraud theory), the apostles knew they were perpetuating a hoax and that not one single word of the Resurrection was true. Nevertheless, in the face of a barbaric death, they spread it around with such a fire of conviction that it changed the world. If the disciples invented a legend, they didn't do a very good job. Legends are full of mythical characters and fantastical events, and they certainly do not include material that could easily be refuted. If the narrator(s) of the legend are woven into it, as are the apostles in the Resurrection story, they tend to insert self-congratulatory stories and are free of embarrassing details. Legends evolve over long periods of time; they do not begin and end in a time and place when and where people can check the story out for themselves. The stuff legends are made of is illustrated in the apocryphal Gospel of Peter, written sometime in the 8th or 9th centuries. This manuscript covers Jesus' trial, death, burial, and Resurrection. Whoever wrote this laid it on really thick, complete with a giant Jesus and a talking cross, as in verses 38 through 42:

> Therefore, having seen this, the soldiers woke up the centurions and elders, for they were also keeping watch. And while they were describing to them the things they had seen, behold, they saw three men coming

out of the tomb, with the two young men supporting the One, and a cross following them. And the head of the two reaching unto to heaven, but the One of whom they led out by the hand, His head reached beyond the heavens. And they heard a voice from heaven asking, "Did you preach to those who sleep?" And a response was heard from the cross saying, "Yes!"

The Gospel accounts of the Resurrection contain no such fantasies. The Gospel accounts are simple eyewitness accounts of a historical event that lack bizarre embellishment. The only event that non-believers would call fantastical is the Resurrection itself, but that occurrence could have been easily refuted if it was not true. There are no mythical characters in the Gospel accounts. Joseph of Arimathea, who assumed responsibility for Jesus' burial, was a rich member of the Jewish Sanhedrin, and according to Matthew, Mark, and John, a secret follower of Jesus. Given his status in the community, Willian Craig notes that "it would be almost inexplicable why Christians would make up a story about a Jewish Sanhedrist who does what is right by Jesus."[9] All characters in the Gospels were real historical figures, still alive when the disciples began preaching, and many still alive when the Gospels were written.

The testimony of the Resurrection occurred at a time and place when people were able to verify or refute it for themselves and were invited to do so by Paul in 1 Corinthians 15:3-8:

> For what I received I passed on to you as of first importance: that Christ died for our sins according to the Scriptures, that he was buried, that he was raised on the third day according to the Scriptures, and that he appeared to Cephas, and then to the Twelve. After that, he appeared to more than five hundred of the brothers and sisters at the same time, most of whom are still living, though some have fallen asleep. Then he appeared to James, then to all the apostles, and last of all he appeared to me also, as to one abnormally born.

Paul is saying to doubters that there are many witnesses to the risen Christ who are still alive and are there to be questioned. He would not have said that if the story was made-up.

The apostles were central figures in the Resurrection narrative, but we see no self-congratulatory stories in their accounts. On the contrary, their accounts contain embarrassing details that refute the notion that the legend theory. The Gospels note that on the night Jesus was arrested the disciples fled in fear and stayed behind locked doors, that Paul (Saul) mercilessly persecuted Christians, and that Peter denied Christ three times. No inventors of legends would paint themselves as cowards, tyrants, and hypocrites. They could have left out such embarrassing details, but chose to tell their story exactly as it happened—a clear indication of truth. Another embarrassing fact is that the empty tomb was discovered by women. Women had such low status among the Jews (and in most other known cultures at the time) that the testimony of the principal witnesses to the empty tomb would be worthless. If the Gospels were relating a legendary story, their writers would surely have claimed that privilege for themselves. The recording of this embarrassing fact adds credence to the fact of the empty tomb. The legend theory can explain the empty tomb and the postmortem appearance of Jesus, but its Achille's heel is that it cannot explain how disheartened, confused, and fearful men became determined and courageous overnight after seeing Jesus. Authors of legends do not have such extraordinary transformations, nor are they willing to die for their deceitful stories.

One reference in the New Testament that used to be called legendary, or at least a piece of poetic license to emphasize the significance of the event, was the darkness during the time Jesus hung on the cross. However, a non-Christian historian named Thallus wrote a book in 52AD in which he made reference to this darkness, which he assumed was caused by a solar eclipse. Then there was the Greek author, Phlegon of Thralles who "reported that in the 202nd Olympiad (i.e., 33 A.D.) there was 'the greatest eclipse of the sun' and that 'it in the sixth hour of the day [i.e., noon] so that stars even appeared in the heavens. There was a great earthquake in Bithynia, and many things were overturned in Nicaea.'"[10] However, it could not have been an eclipse (which lasts a few minutes) because the Bible says that the darkness lasted for 3 hours. A solar eclipse happens only when the moon and the sun are on the same side of the Earth. Jesus' crucifixion happened during Passover, which occurs during a full moon, and for the moon to be full, the moon must be on the opposite side of the Earth. Thus, it could not have been a natural eclipse.

The Hallucination Theory

Secular theories attempting to provide naturalistic accounts of the Resurrection arose in the 18th and 19th centuries. They have been so thoroughly mauled by the historical data that they have all but disappeared from the scholarly world, if not from the amateurs on the Internet. The only theories still held by some staunch naturalists in the scholarly world are psychological in nature. That is, the notion that the apostles experienced some sort of psychologically abnormal experience such as hallucinations, conversion disorder, or bereavement visions. However, few proponents of these ideas have an adequate understanding of the underlying clinical mechanisms of these phenomena. The first of these theories is the hallucination theory.

Hallucinations are rare events that occur in people suffering some kind of preexisting mental problem such as schizophrenia or epilepsy, caused by drugs or some sort of bodily deprivation (food, water, sleep). They tend to occur in people full of excited emotional expectations, and certainly not among those experiencing depression, fear, and anxiety, as the apostles did according to the Gospels. The apostles had no expectations of seeing Jesus alive again after His internment because the death and Resurrection of a messiah is a thoroughly un-Jewish notion. When Mary Magdalene saw Jesus, she thought He was the gardener, and when the disciples heard the report of the women about the empty tomb: "their words seemed to them like nonsense" (Luke 24:11). While the disciples discussed the women's reports the risen Jesus came among them and said "Peace be with you," and "They were startled and frightened, thinking they saw a ghost. He said to them, "Why are you troubled, and why do doubts rise in your minds? Look at my hands and my feet. It is I myself! Touch me and see; a ghost does not have flesh and bones, as you see I have" (Luke 24:36-39). The skeptical apostles had a difficult time accepting the Resurrection and thought that they were seeing a ghost. It was not until they experienced Jesus fully with all their senses that they accepted the bodily Resurrection.

Psychologist Gary Collins notes that: "Hallucinations are individual subjective occurrences. By their very nature only one person can see a given hallucination at a time. They certainly aren't something which can be seen by a group of people. Neither is it possible that one person could somehow induce a hallucination in somebody else."[11] This is a major obstacle to the theory since over a period of 40 days Jesus appeared to numerous people, many of whom became Christians as a result. Furthermore, people routinely deny their hallucinatory experience when others present do not see them, but the apostles maintained their belief that they had seen, touched, spoken, and eaten with the risen Christ, even under torture and imminent death.

Bergeron and Habermas also note that hallucinations are private experiences, and that "collective simultaneous hallucinations, such an explanation is far outside mainstream clinical thought. What are the odds that separate individuals in a group could experience simultaneous and identical psychological phenomena mixed with hallucinations? ...the concept of collective-hallucination is not found in peer reviewed medical and psychological literature."[12] Looking at all medical and psychological causes of hallucinations, they note that the Apostles were not candidates for them. They further note that:

> This would especially be the case with those who prior to these appearances did not venerate Jesus as other than a misguided common man, such as Paul and probably James the brother of Jesus thought. Further, if Jesus' tomb had been found empty, as a majority of scholars

now concur was the case, this would be an additional factor counting against a purely psychiatric hypothesis for the biblical account of Easter.[13]

Hallucinations do not change lives so completely as to create radically new beliefs. After seeing Jesus, talking with Him, and touching His wounds, contrary to their Jewish faith, hundreds came to believe in His message. If every person among the hundreds or thousands—who saw Jesus were hallucinating, we might consider that a miracle in need of a naturalist explanation.

The Conversion Disorder and Bereavement Visions Theories

The term "conversion" was coined by Sigmund Freud who believed certain symptoms not explained by organic brain disease reflect unconscious conflict converting a mental issue, such as repressed guilt, into physical symptoms. The conversion disorder notion was introduced to try to explain the conversion (in the religious sense) of James and Paul, the two disciples that Bergeron and Habermas say were less open to hallucination because they did not venerate Jesus prior to their experience of the Resurrection. The conversion theory posits that both men were guilt-ridden and that guilt manifested itself in bodily symptoms. But there is no indication that James suffered any such symptoms, and although Paul did suffer temporary blindness after Christ appeared to him on the road to Damascus, every indication is that he did not have any guilt whatsoever about his persecution of Christians.[14] The conversion disorder hypothesis is nothing more than dodgy psychoanalysis at a distance.

Hallucinations are experienced as the inability to distinguish what is physically real from what is illusionary, but a vision is an image of someone that the person seeing it knows that the person in the vision does not presently exist, and a vision is not associated with a mental disorder. There are numerous accounts of people experiencing visions of departed loved ones, but that is evidence that the person in the vision is dead, not alive. Nicholas Wright notes that the earliest Christians knew that, and says: "Lots of people have visions of someone they love who has just died... and they had language for it; they would say, 'It's his angel' or 'It's his spirit' or 'his ghost.' They wouldn't say, 'He's been raised from the dead.'"[15] The vision theory is even less plausible than the hallucination hypothesis; would you risk torture and death for something you knew was not real? Bergeron and Habermas conclude "that attempts to explain the disciples' reports of Jesus' Resurrection by subjective, psychiatric hypotheses are fraught with many difficulties. Ultimately, they prove to be clinically implausible and historically unconvincing. The available data point elsewhere and confirm the earliest reports that the disciples' experiences were not merely psychological but transformative experiences of faith."[16]

The transformation of the apostles from cowards to fearless carriers of the message of salvation within a period of days, and their subsequent martyrdom, is proof you can personally relate to. Would you forsake your previous religious beliefs and leave your job, home, and family to travel around the known world, constantly in danger of derision, arrest, torture, and execution for something you knew to be a lie? Plenty of people have died for what they believe in, but not for something they knew to be false because it was a fiction of their own making. Ten of the original disciples died horribly gruesome deaths for what they knew to be true. If you were one of them and knew what you were preaching was a silly fantasy you and your fellow conspirators made up, wouldn't you admit it to save yourself from such a fate? Of course you would, but not one of the disciples did. Neither would you risk all on the basis of a hallucination or a vision.

What if any one of the disciples recanted under threat of torture and death, as we would certainly expect if they knew the Resurrection to be false? Such a recantation would have been devastating to Christianity. Because the early Christian movement existed as closely linked communities, "the news of their recantation would have been widely known among the Christians anyway. This would have caused them to suspect that their faith was worthless and thus to leave the faith, and Christianity would not have survived further persecutions."[17] Michael Licona similarly argues: "We may also expect that a recantation by any of the disciples would have provided ammunition for Christian opponents like Celsus and Lucian in the third quarter of the second century, the former of which wrote against the church while the latter wrote of the Christian movement in a pejorative manner."[18] No such ammunition was ever provided to the enemies of Christianity; a striking testimony to the strength of the Resurrection message and to the faith it inspired in those to whom the Lord appeared.

Almost all historians, philosophers, and theologians—Christian, atheist, agnostic, or persons of a non-Christian faith who have seriously studied the events surrounding the Resurrection—agree that something momentous occurred. Christians agree with Andrew Loke who writes: "The conclusion that Jesus' Resurrection is a case of historical certainty is further supported by the fact that, despite intense scrutiny over the centuries by so many sceptics, the case for Jesus' Resurrection has stood the test of time and that no modern historian has come up with a more convincing explanation."[19] Some secularist scholars have become Christians because of the evidence they have uncovered, others with the same evidence remain skeptical about the biblical message of the Resurrection because in their materialist minds miracles just don't happen. They ask such questions as if the dead Jesus really did rise from the tomb and was allegedly seen by so many people in Jerusalem and elsewhere, why didn't

Secular Attempts to Explain the Resurrection

he reveal himself to the Sanhedrin and throw off the yoke of Rome? That would have settled the whole matter of God's existence, and the world would be a better place. Once again, the answer is that God must maintain epistemic distance from us lest belief be forced on us. This cognitive distance ensures a free choice to accept God or not. However, there is one piece of physical evidence for the literal truth of the Resurrection that I believe is compelling: the "silent witness" of the Shroud of Turin.

Notes

1. In Butt, M., 2002, np.
2. Craig, W., 2008, p. 341.
3. Loke, A., 2020 p. 70.
4. Rhodes, R., 2013, p. 149.
5. Gromacki, G., 2002, p. 72.
6. In Loke, A., 2020, p. 74.
7. Ibid, p. 73.
8. Edwards, W., Gabel, W., & Hosmer, F., 1986, p. 1460.
9. Craig, W., 2010, p. 224.
10. Strobel, L. 1998, p. 85.
11. In Holding, 2010, p.342.
12. Bergeron, J. & Habermas, G., 2015, p.161.
13. Ibid, p. 164.
14. Craig, W., 2010, p. 275.
15. Wright, N., 2008, p. 62.
16. Bergeron, J. & Habermas, G., 2015, p.172.
17. Loke, A., 2020, p. 77.
18. Licona, M., 2010, p. 371.
19. Loke, A., 2020, p. 204.

Chapter 7

The History of the Shroud of Turin

Introduction to the Shroud of Turin

The Shroud of Turin is the most enigmatic and most studied artifact in history. It is a juncture in which revealed and natural theology meet because there are many people—both scientists and non-scientists—who have embraced Christianity on learning what science has to say about it. The Shroud is a piece of sepia-yellow colored ancient linen, 14' 3" long and 3' 7" wide that bears the front and back images of a naked, bearded, crucified man about 5' 10" tall. It has been subjected to so much scrutiny because many believe it to be the burial cloth of Jesus bearing signs of the Resurrection. Because of its religious significance, skeptics have tried for decades to show that is it a medieval forgery. As historian John Walsh put it: "The Shroud is either the most awesome and instructive relic of Christ in existence, or it is one of the most ingenious, most unbelievably clever products of the human mind and hand on record. It is either one or the other; there is no middle ground."[1]

Scholars have been trying to determine the authenticity of the cloth for decades using the most modern technology and techniques from physics, statistics, chemistry, biology, botany, genetics, medical forensics, textile technology, art history, theology, and optical image analysis, but the image defies the most sophisticated investigations as to how it was made (see the full-length front and back photograph of the image below). *Time Magazine* called the image "the riddle of the ages," and *National Geographic* concluded that it is "one of the most perplexing enigmas of modern times... an extraordinary mystery that has defied every effort at solution." This chapter explores the Shroud's vague and semi-legendary historical provenance and the following chapter examines scientific studies that have been conducted on the cloth to determine which of Walsh's alternatives is most plausible: authentic or fake.

As noted previously, scholars have demanded greater proof of the Bible's authenticity than any other ancient documents. It should not surprise anyone that the situation is the same for the Shroud of Turin. Archaeologist William Meacham notes that scientists have demanded an impossible level of proof for the claim that the Shroud is a first-century burial cloth of a crucified man, and that man is Jesus Christ. He also says that it should be subjected to similar tests of authentication as other ancient artifacts: "Clearly, authenticity should be judged on criteria no more and no less stringent than those applied in the usual identification of ancient city sites, royal tombs, manuscripts, etc."[2] Yet tests of authentication of the Shroud have gone way beyond those applied to any other artifact in history. If the Shroud had been any non-religious ancient secular artifact, it would have been accepted as authentic beyond a reasonable doubt by virtue of the multitude of studies of it that have been conducted, even those prior to Meacham's 1983 article. Meacham is aware that there can be no absolute certainty of knowledge, but notes: "in an epistemological framework no stricter than that normally operative for judgements of history and science, the image on the Shroud of Turin can, I submit, be confidently ascribed to the body of Christ."[3] However, we should be glad to see the shroud subjected to tests of authenticity far in excess of those conducted on other artifacts because the claim that it is the burial cloth of Jesus is an extraordinary claim, and extraordinary claims require extraordinary evidence.

Figure 7.1 The Full Front and Back of the Shroud (note the faintness of the image)

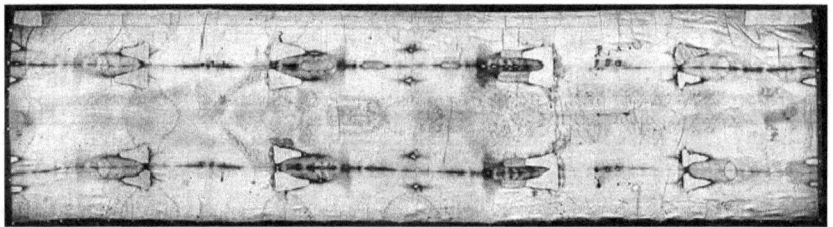

The Shroud and the Image of Edessa

There are two historical periods associated with the Shroud. The first is the period between the crucifixion and its exposition in France in 1357, where it appeared under mysterious circumstances with no documentation as to its provenance. After the Shroud appeared in France its provenance thereafter is well documented, and it now rests in the Cathedral of Saint John the Baptist in the city of Turin. Historical references to a Shroud from the crucifixion to the 14th century are sporadic, but there are a number of early documents that strongly suggest that the Shroud is one and the same as another icon described below as the Image of Edessa. Piecing the story together prior to 1357 is a task for the historical detective who must comb through a maze of circumstantial evidence, carefully scrutinize the above-mentioned documents, and appraise what he or she can from legends and half-legends.

If the Shroud of Turin is the burial cloth of Jesus, the Gospels tell us that it was found by Peter and John in the empty tomb: "Then Simon Peter came, following him, and went into the tomb. He saw the linen cloths lying there, and the face cloth, which had been on Jesus' head, not lying with the linen cloths but folded up in a place by itself. Then the other disciple, who had reached the tomb first, also went in, and he saw and believed" (John 20: 6-8). There must have been something truly remarkable about the shroud itself to have had such an instantaneous effect on Peter, and because it was a physical reminder of Jesus and contained his blood. Given this, we may assume that the apostles did everything they could to protect, conceal, and preserve it because the Roman authorities would certainly have destroyed it if its presence were known as evidence that Jesus had risen. Parenthetically, the finding of these burial cloths is further evidence that no one went to the wrong tomb.

One of the earliest clues tracing the early history of the Shroud is found in the 4th Century document known as *The Doctrine of Addai*, which is allegedly based on material from the state archives of Edessa (modern-day Urfa, Turkey). The *Doctrine* relates to the foundation of Christianity in Edessa, a semi-autonomous state of the Roman Empire during the reign of Emperor Tiberius, located within what is now Turkey. It begins with the story of King Abgar V, who was dying of leprosy and who also suffered from gout. According to the *Doctrine*, Abgar had heard about Jesus' healing powers and sent a letter to Him requesting that He come to Edessa to heal him. One version of this story relates that Abgar sent his secretary, who was also a gifted artist with the message to paint the portrait of Jesus, but the painter "could not manage to follow the changes on the divine countenance and gave up the portrait in despair. So Christ put His napkin against His face and printed His features upon it."[4] The *Doctrine* relates that Jesus responded that He could not come, but after he had gone to his Father in heaven, will send one of his disciples. Thaddaeus (Addai, is the Syriac name for Thaddaeus) went to Edessa to minister to Abgar after Jesus was crucified carrying Jesus' burial cloth. Upon viewing Jesus' face on the cloth, the *Doctrine* tells us that Abgar was instantly healed.[5]

One can dismiss the revelations in *The Doctrine of Addai* as legends, and there certainly have been additions and embellishments to its story. For instance, the story of Jesus imprinting his face on a napkin while He was alive clearly contradicts the version that has Thaddaeus carrying the burial cloth of Jesus to Edessa after His death on the cross. Historian Ilaria Ramelli does say that the Doctrine "might contain some historical traces... even though wrapped in a legendary dress."[6] Nevertheless, there is no other explanation for why Abgar converted to Christianity and lived for another ten years or so, or why Edessa became the first Christian state in history. It is well chronicled that thousands of pilgrims traveled hundreds of miles to see the Image of Edessa. One notable thing about the Image of Edessa is that early references to it describe it as blurred, which also describes the Shroud of Turin. The Edessa cloth was displayed with only the face showing. The Shroud of Turin shows fold marks consistent with a cloth folded in such a way that only the face could be seen (see the fold mark across Jesus' beard in Figure 7.3), making it likely that the Image of Edessa and the Shroud of Turin are the same cloth. When Ma'nu VI became ruler of Edessa in 57AD he reverted to paganism under pressure from Rome. Ma'nu tried to suppress Christianity, but the young church continued to thrive under threat of persecution, but Christians wisely hid the Image and nothing further was heard about it for almost 500 years.[7]

One version of the story relates that the Image was found again in a church hidden in a chest in a secret chamber when the church underwent a major renovation following a devastating flood in 525AD. Another version is that it was discovered by the Bishop of Edessa in 544AD when King Chosroes I of Persia laid an unsuccessful siege to the city.[8] French historian A.M. Dubarle notes that a Syrian hymn celebrating the inauguration of the new cathedral of Edessa, mentions how the marble is comparable to the image made "not by hands;" an obvious reference to the Edessa image: "Its marble is similar to the image that-not-by-hands and its walls are harmoniously covered with it. And for its splendor, all clean and all white, it holds light within itself."[9] Dubarle also quotes Germanus I of Constantinople (715-730) as stating: "There is an image of Christ in the city of Edessa, it is not made by the hands of man and is working amazing wonders. The Lord Himself, after imprinting his own image on a soudárion, sent to Abgar, Toparch of the Edessenians' city, by the intermediary Thaddeus the Apostle, the image which maintains his human physiognomy and healed Abgar's illness."[10]

Edessa surrendered to Muslim rule in 639, but the Image remained there under Muslim protection. Both Christian and Muslim sources relate that Muslims treated the image as a religious icon of the Prophet, Jesus, but they did not believe it to be the image of the risen Christ because Islam rejects the Resurrection. Such was the depth of belief in the image as the true likeness of Christ that Byzantine Emperor Lecapenus sent an army of 80,000 men to capture it and bring it to Constantinople in 944. The Byzantine general, John Curcuas, informed the emir that he would not lay siege to the city and offered the Muslim rulers the return of 200 high-ranking Muslim prisoners, twelve thousand pieces of silver, and a promise of peace in exchange for the Image. The Muslims did not want to release something so venerated by Christians, nor did the Christian inhabitants of Edessa want it to leave the city. After a long series of negotiations, the Muslim rulers decided that it was wise to make the exchange, and the Image was taken to Constantinople.[11] Edessa was conquered by Christians in 1097 during the First Crusade but was subsequently reconquered by a Muslim army in 1144.

The Shroud was allegedly stolen by French and Venetian knights, whose greed surpassed their piety, in the plunder of Constantinople during the Fourth Crusade in 1204. Working in the Vatican archives in 2008, Barbara Frale found documentary evidence that the Knights Templar held custody of the Shroud during the 13th and 14th centuries, and used it in initiation ceremonies.[12] Another fairly reliable pre-14th century account "is provided by Robert de Clari, knight of Picardy and a chronicler of the Fourth Crusade. De Clari describes seeing a shroud similar to the one at Turin in the monastery of Our Lady Saint Mary of Blachernae in Constantinople: "stretched up every Friday, so that one could well see on it the figure of our Lord."[13] Frale also noted that Arnaut Sabbatier testified in the trial process of the Templars that in 1287 he kissed the feet of a figure of a man imprinted on "a long linen cloth."[14] The first undisputed fact about the Shroud is that it was exhibited in Lirey, France, in 1356 by Geoffrey De Charny, whose ancestors were leaders within the Knights Templar. This may be taken as circumstantial evidence that the Templars held the Shroud prior to this. It was later entrusted to the royal family of Savoy, who brought it to its current location in Turin in 1578. The Shroud has remained in the Cathedral of Saint John the Baptist ever since, except for brief periods when it was removed for safekeeping during times of war.

Is the Image of Edessa and the Shroud of Turin the Same Cloth?

When the Image of Edessa arrived in Constantinople in 944, a sermon was preached by Gregory Referendarius, Archdeacon of Hagia Sophia, on the occasion of its arrival. In it, Gregory said:

> And so, what exactly is it? By the simple touching to the face of Christ, an image of his form was made, so that people would not think in a dangerous or perilous way that it never actually existed and has been invented. And so even if nobody wishes to help me in this, I will step forward to state that it is not necessary to postpone good things. I will now therefore bring forward the witnesses, not in a magnificent style with polished words, lest the cross of Christ be rendered vain, but rather with simple letters and words, so that even if my own words show I am not an elegant writer, my knowledge will show I am not ignorant.[15]

While in Constantinople, the Image was contained in the great cathedral of Hagia Sophia, which was supposedly built specifically to house and preserve it. There remains controversy over whether the Image of Edessa and the Shroud are one and the same because the Image is most commonly referred to as a small cloth showing only the face of Christ, whereas the Shroud of Turin is a large linen cloth showing the whole body. That the Image of Edessa and the Shroud of Turin are probably one and the same, has been most strenuously argued by historian Ian Wilson.[16] Archaeologist Virginia Bortin notes that although the Edessa cloth appears as only a face:

Wilson quotes a 6th-century text which refers to the cloth as 'doubled in four.' When the Turin shroud is thus folded, only the head can be seen, and it appears to be curiously disembodied. [Wilson] postulates that the shroud's full figure was not apparent until the cloth reached Constantinople. Before that time, it had been folded, mounted, and displayed as a facial image-perhaps to obscure its use as a burial shroud, since early Christians feared the cloth might be destroyed by Jews, who believed it to be impure.[17]

The Jewish notion that burial cloths are unclean and untouchable might explain why the Shroud was displayed in a wide frame, which allowed room for a much larger cloth folded inside, with only the face showing. This is consistent with the fold marks clearly visible on the Shroud (see Figure 7.3). It may have also been displayed this way to hide the nakedness of Christ.

Daniel Scavone adds further evidence for the hypothesis, noting that the first reference to the Shroud itself being in Constantinople occurred in 958: "Yet there exists no record of the arrival of the Shroud. The most plausible conclusion, hypothesized by Ian Wilson... is that it was the Mandylion [an alternate word for the Edessa Image] unfolded in 958. In any case, awareness of the full-body image on cloth had reached Britain by the twelfth century."[18] That is two centuries before its first undisputed documented appearance in France. Scavone also notes that after the Image of Edessa's appearance in Constantinople, there is no further reference to it, possibly because after the Image's true dimensions were known after its unfolding, it was recognized as the Shroud. As I said, this is historical detective work rather than history proper, but I think it more than plausible that the Image of Edessa and the Shroud of Turin are the same cloth.

The Sudarium of Oviedo

There is also a link between the Shroud of Turin and a relic held in the Cathedral El Salvador in Oviedo, Spain, known as the Sudarium of Oviedo. This link is strong because the Sudarium's history is well documented from at least 614AD and lacks the ambiguity surrounding the provenance of the Shroud. Because the Sudarium's history is well documented, it is not necessary to reiterate it here. The evidence is also strong because it has been scientifically compared to the Shroud with amazing results. The Sudarium is a cloth measuring approximately 33 by 21 inches. Notice again that John 20: 6-7 tells us: "Then Simon Peter came along behind him and went straight into the tomb. He saw the strips of linen lying there, as well as the cloth that had been wrapped around Jesus' head. The cloth was still lying in its place, separate from the linen." These words clearly both link and differentiate the face cloth and the full-body shroud found in Christ's tomb and are what we have come to call the Sudarium of Oviedo and the Shroud of Turin.

Unlike the Shroud, there is no image on the Sudarium; only stains are visible to the naked eye. When examined scientifically, both the Sudarium and the Shroud have been shown to contain AB-type bloodstains in identical patterns. When the image of the Shroud is placed on the stains of the Sudarium, through a method of image comparison known as the Polarized Image Overlay Technique, it has been found that there are an astounding 130 marks of congruence between stains on the Sudarium and the bloodstains on the man's face on the Shroud. Twenty-five points of congruence is usually accepted as conclusive proof of the same origin (as, for example, in fingerprinting).[19] This exceeds the accepted level of proof in science and in the criminal justice system by more than five times. The identical blood type and the large number of marks of congruence render it beyond a reasonable doubt that the two cloths were on the same body.

The Hungarian Pray Manuscript

Skeptics do not accept the admittedly sparse history of the Shroud's early provenance. Partly because of its scantiness, and partly based on the hypothesis that the Shroud is a medieval artifact made sometime in the 13th or 14th centuries. However, another piece of evidence that argues against this theory is one of the illustrations in the Hungarian Pray Manuscript (or Codex) named after the Jesuit priest György Pray. The Codex contains two miniatures depicting the Anointing at the top and Three Marys at the Tomb of Christ at the bottom. This is a significant piece of evidence that the Shroud was in Constantinople prior to 1204 because the Pray Manuscript is firmly dated to the early 1190s. The illustration depicts a naked Jesus, hands across the pelvis, with no thumbs visible, being anointed and wrapped in a burial cloth.

Comparisons of the Pray depiction in Figure 7.2 and the Shroud, one can see that they bear many similarities. The fabric illustrated in the Pray Manuscript has a herringbone weave, a technique unknown in medieval Europe, identical to the Shroud. There and several other things in the illustration, including, "a series of four holes arranged in an 'L' shape, whose position and shape correspond to those of the so-called 'L-holes' in the Turin Shroud"[20] that leads art experts to conclude that the artist copied it from the Shroud. To account for the similarities, and because they are aware that the Pray manuscript precedes the known documented provenance of the Shroud in France, skeptics turn the table around to claim that whoever the genius was they alleged forged the Shroud copied it from Pray Manuscript. Such a preposterous notion might be entertained if those putting it forward could offer some realistic method by which the image got onto the Shroud which, as we shall see, is something that scientists have been trying to discover for 125 years.

Figure 7.2 The Hungarian Pray Manuscript

Images: Acheiropoieta and Photographs

It should be noted that because Exodus 20:4 commands a ban on creating graven images, some Christians, not wanting to be accused of idolatry, did not want the Image displayed, and even declared it false. This has been a repeated debate among Christian theologians, particularly among Catholic and Protestant theologians. But the ban is on icons "made by [human] hands," not on acheiropoieta, which are icons that have come into existence miraculously; authored by Godly powers. Petri notes that acheiropoieta have "the power to bypass the ban on man-made images," and that "Combining qualities of icon and relic, the acheiropoietic are perfect renderings of their subject; in fact they turn out to be their subject."[21] That is, the Divine Artist who created the Shroud created an image of Himself.

Figure 7.3 Positive and Negative Images of the Shroud

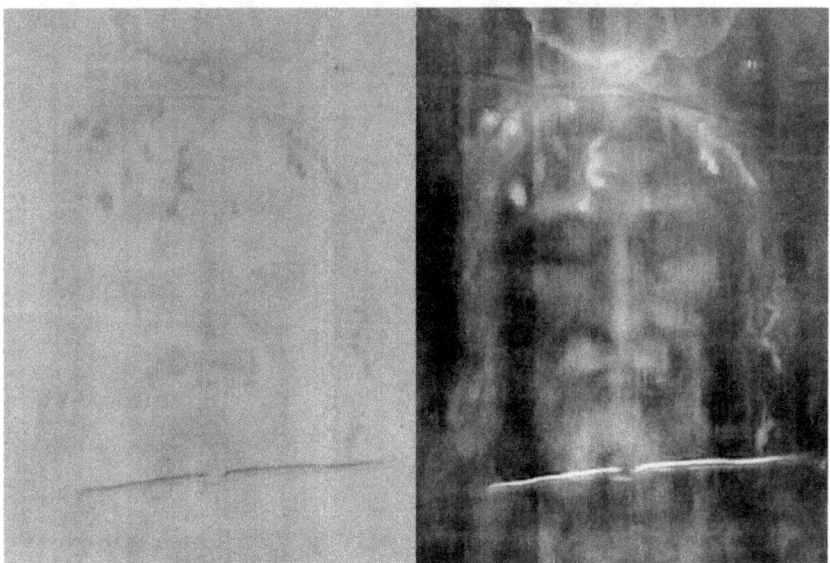

    Positive as Negative Image   **Negative as Positive Image**

The Shroud of Turin stirred little controversy outside of theology other than the "graven image" issue when it was simply a relic in a Turin cathedral. It was very rarely seen and virtually unknown outside of Church circles, but this changed in 1898 when it was first photographed. The scientific quest to either authenticate or falsify the Shroud as the burial sheet of Jesus began with these photographs taken by Turin lawyer and amateur photographer Secondo Pia.[22] Pia was astonished when he viewed the negative on the plate of his photograph. Instead of showing the vague outline of a bearded man, the negative was sharp and detailed, showing the image of a terribly tortured body. This reveals that the Shroud Image was seen down the centuries as etched in negative form (an image where the light values are reversed), just like a photographic negative, but on *non-photographic linen*. Pia's photographs had created a negative of the "negative" of the Shroud, which mysteriously produced a normal positive image with the correct light and dark contrasts. This detailed negative of a ghostly positive image was somehow imprinted on a cloth only to be revealed by photography. But photography was not invented until the early 19th century, and a photograph cannot be inscribed on linen. Figure 7.3 contrasts the vague photographic positive image of the head of the man in the Shroud as seen with the naked eye on the left with the clear photographic negative image on the right.

Notes

1. In Fanti, G. 2012, p. 2506.
2. Meacham, W. 1983, p. 284.
3. Ibid. p. 309.
4. Runciman, S., 1931, p. 240.
5. Green, M., 1969.
6. Ramelli, I., 2011, p. 110.
7. Tribbe, F. 2006.
8. Runciman, S., 1931.
9. Dubarle, A. M., 1985, pp. 99-100.
10. Ibid, p. 81.
11. Runciman, S., 1931.
12. Thavis, J., 2009.
13. Bortin, V., 1980, p. 115.
14. Scavone, D., 2010, p. 6.
15. Guscin, M., 2009, p.73.
16. Wilson, I., 1978.
17. Bortin, V. 1980, p. 115.
18. Scavone, D., 2010, p. 7.
19. In Tribbe, F., 2006, p. 166.
20. Flury-Lemberg, M., 2009, p. 43.
21. Petri, G., 2018, p. 154.
22. Tribbe, F. 2006.

Chapter 8

Scientific Testing of the Shroud of Turin

The Shroud of Turin Research Project

It was noted in the previous chapter that the early history of the Shroud is historical detective work; so is the science of the Shroud. It is obviously not an experimental science in the sense that scientists can experiment with cadavers to try to determine how a dead body can create an image of itself on linen. What we are looking at in this chapter is forensic science revealing the secrets the Shroud itself can reveal to us. This is analogous to forensic science lab work conducted when trying to uncover the person who committed a particular murder. Forensic scientists determine the time and manner of death, take DNA samples, analyze pollen and fibers found at the murder scene, and report their results to detectives. Detectives then follow the evidence where it leads to rule out suspects and hopefully arrive at the correct conclusion as to who the true culprit is. This is how scientific research is conducted on the Shroud: follow the evidence where it leads while trying to eliminate bias or presupposition. Results of scientific research are then published so that others can conduct their own analyses to see if they arrive at the same conclusion, or see if they can resolve discrepancies or resolve some issue left dangling by the original research protocol. This is how any science, including the science of the Shroud, is conducted.

Scientific-quality photographic negatives taken in 1978, 2002, and 2008 reveal extraordinary details of contusions and anatomical detail that modern pathologists have described as perfectly consistent with crucifixion. The 2008 image is composed of 1,600 credit-card-sized images for a total image of 12.8 billion pixels of high-resolution color scans of extraordinarily high definition.[1] The photographs reveal that the intensity of the image varies with the expected distance between the body and the cloth; that is, the closer the draping of the Shroud to the body, the more intense is the body image. The photographs show that the man in the image was crucified in the classical Roman way with wounds that are consistent with Gospel accounts of Jesus' suffering. There are over 100 whip marks on every portion of the body, bloodstains forming a circle around the top of his head consistent with the crown of thorns, severely bruised knees consistent with Jesus falling on the way to his crucifixion, holes, and bloodstains in wrists and feet consistent with having been caused by large nails, and bloodstains around a large side wound consistent with the account of Jesus' side being pierced by a spear. Furthermore, and compatible with the biblical account, the man in the Shroud did not have broken legs, which was typically done to speed asphyxia and death, as was done to the thieves crucified on either side of Jesus, but not done to Jesus because He was already dead.

Many scientists have examined higher quality photos of the Shroud taken after Pia's, but the Shroud itself was not examined invasively until an international team of scientists led by nuclear physicists Tom D'Muhala and John Jackson formed the Shroud of Turin Research Project (STURP). In 1978, a STURP team of 52 scientists with specialties in computer technology, hematology, physics, chemistry, spectroscopy, and X-ray analysis was granted five days of access to the Shroud. Using millions of dollars of sophisticated equipment, STURP scientists studied the Shroud in shifts around the clock for those five days. STURP members included Christians, Jews, atheists, and agnostics, a few saying that with their sophisticated equipment, they "would doubtless prove its spuriousness." STURP continued examining its data and published many of its results in scientific journals and proceedings. In its 1981 final report, STURP wrote:

> No pigments, paints, dyes or stains have been found on the fibrils. X-ray, fluorescence and microchemistry on the fibrils preclude the possibility of paint being used as a method for creating the image. Ultra Violet and infrared evaluation confirm these studies. Computer image enhancement and analysis by a device known as a VP-8 image analyzer show that the image has unique, three-dimensional information encoded in it. Microchemical evaluation has indicated no evidence of any spices, oils, or any biochemicals known to be produced by the body in life or in death. It is clear that there has been a direct contact of the Shroud with a body, which explains certain features such as scourge marks, as well as the blood. However, while this type of contact might explain some of the features of the torso, it is totally incapable of explaining the image of the face with the high resolution that has been amply demonstrated by photography. We can conclude for now that the Shroud image is that of a real human form of a scourged, crucified man. It is not the product of an artist. The blood stains are composed of hemoglobin and also give a positive test for serum albumin. The image is an ongoing mystery and until further chemical studies are made, perhaps by this group of scientists, or perhaps by some scientists in the future, the problem remains unsolved.[2]

Carbon-14 Dating of the Shroud

Scientists hate mysteries, so in 1985 experts in carbon-14 (^{14}C) dating met to review protocols regarding the radiocarbon dating of the Shroud. Carbon-14 is a weakly radioactive isotope of carbon-12 that slowly decays over thousands of years. Because the carbon dating process is destructive, only small samples of the object to be dated are used. The most important of the several protocols of carbon dating is that a sample must be representative of the whole item. That is, for a large item such as the Shroud, one cannot take a snippet from one site and assume that it is representative of the whole. Consistent with normal sampling procedures, scientists were supposed to cut seven samples from different areas of the cloth. However, because the Church objected to multiple sampling, in 1988, a single postage-stamp-size sample was cut from the lower-left corner of the Shroud and divided into three subsamples for analyses at the University of Arizona, Oxford University, and the Federal Technical Institute in Switzerland.

Much to the surprise of Shroud scientists, researchers announced that the average of their tests resulted in an age of between 1260 and 1390AD for the Shroud. This was such a surprise given all the other scientific and historical evidence dating it to the first century. If the Shroud is only about 800 years old, then it must be a forgery and we either have to discard mountains of other evidence or conclude that something was amiss with the carbon dating. Christopher Ramsey, head of the Oxford team that conducted the 1988 dating made this point: "There is a lot of other evidence that suggests to many that the shroud is older than the radiocarbon dates allow, and so further research is certainly needed... to arrive at a coherent history of the shroud which takes into account and explains all of the available scientific and historical information."[3]

There is no question as to the scientific pedigree of those who conducted the dating, and nothing is inherently wrong with the ^{14}C testing method. It is the tireless workhorse of archaeology and associated sciences that allows scientists to determine the age of objects containing organic material. Ordinary carbon (^{12}C) has six protons and six neutrons and is thus stable. Carbon-14 has two extra neutrons and is thus slightly unstable (radioactive). Carbon-14 is constantly being created by the interaction of neutrons created by cosmic rays with nitrogen-14 in the atmosphere. The resulting ^{14}C then combines with atmospheric oxygen to form radioactive carbon dioxide, which is absorbed by plants during photosynthesis. Animals acquire ^{14}C by eating plants, and when animals or plants die, they no longer exchange carbon with the environment. From that point on, the amount of ^{14}C contained in them begins to decrease as it undergoes radioactive decay. Ordinary carbon-12 does not decay, so objects containing carbon can be dated by measuring the ^{12}C/^{14}C ratio. The older the object, the less ^{14}C is detected relative to ^{12}C. Thus, carbon dating measures residual radioactivity. Carbon-14 has a half-life of about 5,730 years; that is, the period after which half of a given sample's ^{14}C will have decayed. In other words, after 5,730 years, 50% of the original ^{14}C will remain; after 11,460 years, 25% will remain, and after 17,190 years (three half-lives), 12.5% will remain.

As noted above, among the problems faced in the proper dating of the Shroud was the cloth sampling. It was not representative of the whole, but rather of the so-called "Reas threads" and the so-called "Holland cloth" from the backing of the cloth. The Shroud was damaged by a fire in the Sainte Chapelle, Chambéry, and patched up in 1532 with the Holland cloth. Some have claimed that the fire altered the cloth's carbon content, leading to false dating. Ray Rogers, a thermal chemist at the Los Alamos National Laboratory, was skeptical of theories casting doubt on the ^{14}C dates. According to Philip Ball: "Rogers thought that he would be able to 'disprove [the] theory in five minutes.'"[4] He went about this task using another way of dating plant-based material—the degradation of lignin to vanillin. Lignin is an organic polymer that constitutes the cell walls of land plants and degrades at a known rate over time into vanillin. Where there is lignin in a sample of cloth, it will test positive for vanillin. Rogers tested Reas threads and Holland cloth from the same areas as the 1988 radiocarbon dating study. The medieval threads tested positive for vanillin, but the main body of the Shroud does not have any vanillin, which indicates a much older age than the known medieval threads tested against it. Rogers concludes:

> If the shroud had been produced between A.D. 1260 and 1390, as indicated by the radiocarbon analyses, lignin should be easy to detect. A linen produced in A.D. 1260 would have retained about 37% of its vanillin in 1978. The Raes threads, the Holland cloth, and all other medieval linens gave the test for vanillin wherever lignin could be observed on growth nodes. The disappearance of all traces of vanillin from the lignin in the shroud indicates a much older age than the radiocarbon laboratories reported.... A determination of the kinetics of vanillin loss suggests that the shroud is between 1300- and 3000-years old.[5]

Rogers' study did not directly address the question of whether the 1532 fire could have altered the Shroud's carbon content, only that the dated samples are distinct from the main cloth. This brings up the issue of sample contamination. A study of the textile weaving and surface contaminants on the same areas Rogers tested conducted by chemists Sue Benford and Joe Marino also shows they are chemically distinct from the main body of the Shroud. Benford and Marino also showed that some of the threads woven into the samples are medieval cotton and not linen as in the main cloth of the Shroud. If you date two different threads from two different time periods, you will arrive at a date that gives their weighted average. Given the historical evidence that the cloth was mended after the fire of 1532, and if about 60% of the carbon dating sample consisted of threads from the mending, then the Shroud could be dated to the first century AD. Benford and Marino were among the first to suggest that charring caused by the 1532 fire could have increased the carbon content of the cloth.[6] Research has shown that compared to non-charred material from the same sample, the charring of cellulose material increases its ^{12}C content between 20 and 30%.[7] If this is the case with the Shroud, the carbon dating would have been significantly skewed, showing a higher ^{12}C content relative to ^{14}C, and thus a later date.

We have to conclude that the medieval dates given for the Shroud must be a function of poor sampling since the dating technique itself is not in question. I have done enough studies myself to know that "Garbage in, garbage out" has to be the watchword when dealing with samples. For instance, live snails in their shells have been dated to 26,000 years ago; a freshly killed seal to 1,300 years, and a linen handkerchief known to be less than 50 years old was given an age of 350 years.[8] The best advice regarding how we should respond to the 1988 carbon dating is given by archaeologist Eugenia Nitowski, who stated: "In any form of inquiry or scientific discipline, it is the weight of evidence which must be considered conclusive. In archaeology, if there are ten lines of evidence, carbon dating being one of them, and it conflicts with the other nine, there is little hesitation to throw out the carbon date as inaccurate due to unforeseen contamination."[9]

The Mysteries of the Image

The greatest scientific mystery of the Shroud is how the image was imprinted because for more than a century all mechanisms that have been proposed to explain it have failed. In this sense, the 1988 dating results are a good thing because they provided further stimulus for more scientists to become interested in the Shroud. For instance, the Shroud has been examined extensively by a device called the VP-8 image analyzer and found to contain 3-dimensional information. That is, when a photographic negative of the Shroud (really a positive, since the Shroud itself is a negative) is revealed, an accurate three-dimensional representation of the man on the Shroud is seen. Ordinary flat paintings and photographs cannot reveal 3D likenesses without distortion because the darkness in 2D images does not correspond correctly to depth. That is, no matter how you move around when looking at a photograph or painting, you won't see it in profile, but if you have a statue, you could move around and view it from all angles. How remarkable is it that the Shroud contains the only flat image in existence that contains perfect three-dimensional information? Of course, the Shroud itself is two-dimensional, and its 3D information is imperceptible without a modern VP-8 analyzer. What the Shroud has mysteriously done is retain information about the distance the cloth was from parts of the body it rested on as well as with parts of the body that it had no direct contact with. We can get 3D images from the Shroud because the image is highly correlated with cloth-body distance intensity and this distance correlation reveals a precise mathematical order in the image's structure. Many ingenious experiments have been made to duplicate the Shroud's 3D information with other 2D images without success. If teams of scientists using all sorts of modern computerized photographic technology cannot duplicate the Shroud's 3D information, what are the chances that a medieval artist could?[10]

We see from the positive image (the one that looks like a negative) of the photograph on the left of Figure 7.3, that the image is extremely superficial. The ideal length to view it is 6 to 10 feet; because of the faintness of the image, it disappears as you get closer to it. The image is definitely contained on a linen cloth hand-woven in a manner consistent with the ancient Palestinian weave and is of a man scourged, and crowned with thorns. Multiple studies have shown that the image could not have gotten there by paint, dye, or stain. This would show up in chemical analysis, and the cloth shows no clumping or cracking along the Shroud's fold lines, as it would if some medium was applied to it by a forger. The depth of the image is perfectly uniform throughout; an utterly impossible feat for any painting. Moreover, the discoloration is only on the top one or two fibrils of a thread (a typical thread contains between 100 and 200 fibrils), which amounts to the thickness of about one percent of a single thread, or a discoloration of 0.2 microns of fiber (0.2 microns = 0.00000078 inches).[11] The technology to duplicate this did not exist in medieval times, nor does it exist today.

The original STURP team noted that the image on the Shroud could not be explained scientifically, but hypothesized that it may have been caused by an extremely short and intense burst of energy from the body wrapped in the Shroud that resulted in the dehydration and oxidation of the cellulose fibers of the linen.[12] Physicist Paulo De Lazzaro noted that the UV light necessary to reproduce the image: "exceeds the maximum power released by all ultraviolet light sources available today. The time for such a burst would be shorter than one forty-billionth of a second, and the intensity of the ultraviolet light would have to be around several billion watts."[13] Impossible you say, but such unimaginable energy and precision can actually be achieved today. Using a commercially available paper-printed image of the head of the man in the Shroud as a template, a group of physicists achieved a passable 2D reproduction on a linen sheet using an infrared femtosecond laser.[14] Femtosecond lasers deliver infrared pulses of power of up to 100 billion watts. If such power were to be applied for even a second, the entire cloth would be instantly vaporized. Each "dark" pixel of the digitized photo the scientists used was targeted with 20 pulses from the laser for one femtosecond. One femtosecond is a *millionth* of a *billionth* of a second. Putting this in perspective; there are more femtoseconds in one second than there are seconds in three years. As for the amount of energy involved; 100 billion watts is enough energy to power one billion 100-watt light bulbs.

The making of an image this way is a remarkable feat of science, demonstrating what the STURP team hypothesized in 1981. The researchers stated that their image resulted in the accelerated dehydration and oxidation of the cellulose fibers of the linen. However, the attained image is only a picture on linen that approximates the extremely superficial depth of the Shroud image. Taking a photograph of the image yields only a negative plate that looks exactly like a negative, and not like the positives produced by the negatives of the Shroud. Also, unlike the Shroud, the image does not contain 3D information. Not to take anything away from what these scientists achieved, but the image produced by this marvelous technology is still just an image on linen. The Shroud itself is much more than an image in that it contains 3D information, blood stains, skin debris, hair, ancient pollen, and a bone fragment. There is no combination of physical, chemical, and biological methods known to science that can account for the totality of secrets that the Shroud has revealed over the last 125 years.

Blood, Forensic Pathology, and Pollen Evidence

Human AB+ blood is found on the Shroud and has been extensively studied. Di Lascio and colleagues note: "The reddish stains on the archaeological cloth known as the Shroud of Turin give the appearance of blood stains and independent forensic analyses confirmed that they contain specific blood components, including immunoglobulin, hemoglobin, bilirubin, and albumin, which are consistent with the presence of real blood."[15] DNA has been extracted from the blood, but it is much too contaminated to be of use because hundreds of people have touched the Shroud over the centuries. In a 42-page analysis of the postmortem blood on the Shroud, Adrie van der Hoeven noted that it must have gotten unto the Shroud before the image was formed because when blood was removed from the image the linen under it was whiter than the surrounding areas. This shows conclusively that the blood was applied first and the discoloration of the fibers on the Shroud came later. Van der Hoeven concluded:

> A medieval artist most probably would not have been able to imprint or paint the realistic-looking pinkish red bloodstains in the right anatomical locations on the cloth before he or she would somehow

produce the still not reproduced body image. Besides, the artist would have to have used an ancient and most probably starched and madder-dyed fine linen cloth for this implausible procedure. The medieval-looking result of the radiocarbon-dating of the Shroud, performed on a single sample cut from a corner of the Shroud in 1988, is not an accurate result as the reported radiocarbon ages of the subsamples were statistically shown to be mutually inconsistent.[16]

French forensic pathologist Pierre Barbet was one of the first medical experts to examine the anatomical evidence from the Shroud. He even used cadavers to experiment with aspects of crucifixion. He noted that nailing by the hands, as depicted in paintings of the crucifixion down the centuries could not hold an adult male body, and noted that nailing through the wrist causes median nerve injury that results in palm-ward contraction of the thumb as shown in the Shroud and the Hungarian Pray Manuscript. Like so many experts before him, Barbet was a confirmed skeptic regarding the Shroud's authenticity, but his investigation resulted in him being so impressed with the anatomical accuracy of the Shroud's image that he wrote:

> I am a surgeon ... well-versed in anatomy which I taught for a long time; I lived for thirteen years in close contact with corpses, and have spent the whole of my career examining the anatomy of the living. The idea that an artist of the fourteenth century could have conceived, let alone painted or stained these negative images is sufficient to disgust any physiologist, any surgeon ... This image is enough proof that nobody has touched the Shroud except the Crucified Himself.[17]

Using sophisticated optical microscopy and spectroscopy that allows scientists to analyze elements on areas as small as a nanometer (that's 0.000000039 inches) in diameter with high magnitudes in the depth of focus, Lucotte, and Thomasset examined microscopic particles from a sticky-tape sample from the Shroud and discovered a small nasal bone/cartilage piece, probably resulting from blunt trauma. Their finding points to yet another piece of evidence for the authenticity of the Shroud. The bone/cartilage fragment: "was intensively studied for, colour, thickness, surface morphology and ultrastructure, and for its organic and mineral compositions. Presence of such an osseous [consisting of or turned into bone] remain on the Face adds new substantial material (other than red blood cells, skin debris and one hair, already published) to the knowledge of the Man whose body is imprinted on the Turin Shroud."[18]

The species of microscopic pollen found on the Shroud points to its first-century provenance. Using sticky tape samples from the Shroud, criminologist Max Frei extracted samples of plant pollen, some of which grow exclusively in

Israel, indicating that some time in its existence it had been exposed to the air there. Of the 58 pollen specimens on the fabric, 75% were from plants indigenous to Palestine, and only 17 were from plants that are also found in France and Italy.[19] The pollen of a particular species of thistle was found in abundance on the cloth near the man's shoulders, which may have been the thistle from which the biblical crown of thorns was plaited. Pollen grains of this species were also found in the Sudarium of Oviedo, providing further evidence that the Sudarium and the Shroud touched the same body. Botanist Avinoam Danin of The Hebrew University of Jerusalem commented on these findings in the XVI International Botanical Congress: "There is no way that similar patterns of blood stains, probably of the identical blood type, with the same type of pollen grains, could not be synchronic covering the same body...The pollen association and the similarities in the blood stains in the two cloths provide clear evidence that the shroud originated before the eighth century."[20]

Investigating the compounds of burial ointments and pollen from the first-century Hebrew and medieval funeral practices, botanist M. Boi concluded they could not have come from the medieval era. "Rather, the pollen discovered in this relic [the Shroud] could be from the could be from the compounds of early burial ointments, suggesting that its origins lie in the first century AD. It is not difficult for pollen to stay attached to fibres for a long time, but the attachment can be even stronger when the pollen is combined with greasy botanical substances, such as those applied to the body after death, or those adhering to a burial cloth."[21] Boi then added that this "validates the theory that the corpse kept in the Shroud received a funeral and burial with all the honour and respect that was customary in the Hebrew tradition."[22] Finally, particles of an uncommon variety of limestone have been found on the Shroud's fibers on the feet of the image. The fibers were matched by optical crystallography with samples of limestone from ancient tombs in and near Jerusalem and they matched very closely. This limestone is found in limestone caves in and around Israel, but not in Europe.[23]

What are we to Conclude?

According to skeptics, the evidence against miracles grows proportional to the expansion of scientific understanding, but the more science has explored natural processes, the more puzzling, and miraculous, the image on the Shroud has become. As discussed earlier, the hypothesis that the image was caused by an extremely short and intense burst of energy from the body resulting in the dehydration and oxidation of the cellulose fibers of the linen was partially confirmed by a team of physicists. However, it involved highly sophisticated modern technology utilizing an almost unimaginable level of energy (100 billion watts) and briefness of time (a millionth of a billionth of a second). This feat did not violate any natural law, but it certainly does not cohere with Hume's "regularity of experience," since there is no other burial cloth in existence that has left an imprint of a corpse on it. There is no known phenomenon that occurs naturally; that is, without intelligent input, that involves such energy applied for such a brief time. Additionally, the scientifically produced image does not come close to reproducing all the information contained in the Shroud; only the input of a supremely supernatural intelligence applying *His* laws of nature could have done that.

Is the Shroud the authentic burial cloth of Jesus or an unbelievably clever fake? Assume that it is a painting for a moment; ignoring the fact that this has been entirely ruled out of court. Because the image disappears as you get closer than six feet to it, the genius who painted it must have had seriously long arms to see what he was painting. To begin his forgery, he would have to first acquire a burial cloth of the right material and weave type used in Jerusalem at the time of Jesus. He would then have to salt it with pollen found only in what is now Israel, limestone found in caves only in Jerusalem and surrounding areas, place bloodstains in just the right areas, and plant all the other debris on the shroud. Of course, he would have had to have had an electron microscope to see the debris. Since he could not see these things, he could not have added them, why would he, since if he couldn't see it no one else could? He would have to know about negative images centuries before photography existed and paint an image in the finest detail that perfectly reverses all light and dark shading as in a photographic negative. He would then have to paint an anatomically correct tortured body using knowledge of medical pathology unknown before the twentieth century. He would have to paint blood flows that perfectly agreed with details of death by crucifixion that only a trained forensic pathologist would know. Going against the grain of conventional portraits of the crucifixion, he would somehow have to know that the nails went through the wrists rather than the hands. This caused the thumbs to cling tightly to the hand, as seen in the Shroud and the Hungarian Pray Manuscript. He would have to achieve all this, and more, and then penetrate the cloth only on the top two fibrils (about 1/10 the width of a human hair) of the threads uniformly across the entirety of the image. Naturalistically impossible? You bet!

If the Shroud was made by purely naturalistic means, why don't we see other examples of an image of a corpse encoded on a piece of fabric? Not only that but an image of a crucified man that comports exactly with a man tortured and crucified in the way the Bible describes. The only reasonable conclusion is the one Barrie Schwortz, an orthodox Jew and one of the world's leading experts on the Shroud, arrived at: "The most plausible explanation to me for the Shroud, both because of the science and my own personal background as a Jew, is that it was the cloth that was used to wrap Jesus' body."[24] The science of the Shroud has enriched the faith of millions and stimulated an enormous amount of scientific work. Although I consider the Shroud a silent witness to the Resurrection of Jesus Christ, a solid case for the Resurrection can be made with or without it. Science says the man of the Shroud died a violent death by crucifixion and that all the marks of suffering found on the Shroud correspond exactly with the Gospel accounts of Jesus' torment, but science can't tell us that the man was Jesus. Science has shown conclusively that the image on the Shroud could not possibly have been made by the hand of man, but may never uncover the totality of the mystery of the Shroud. If it is a material trace of the moment of Resurrection—and I don't see what else it could possibly be—then it is evidence of a world-transforming miracle. By definition, a miracle lies beyond the methods of science. Science has been able to say with absolute certainty what the Shroud is *not* (a man-made forgery), but not what it *is* at its deepest level; that's for the theologians.

Notes

1. Schneider, R., 2008.
2. STURP, 1981.
3. In Ramesh, C., 2010, p. 56.
4. Ball, P., 2005, np.
5. Rogers, R., 2005, pp. 191-192.
6. Benford, S., & Marino, J., 2008.
7. Hajaligol, M., Waymack, B., & Kellogg, D. 2001.
8. Tribbe, F., 2006, p 275.
9. In Wilson, I., 1991, pp. 178-179.
10. Tribbe, F., 2006.
11. Fanti, G., & Maggiolo, R. 2004.
12. Fanti, G., 2012.
13. In Longnecker, D., 2015, np.
14. Di Lazzaro, P., Murra, D., Santoni, A., et al, 2010.
15. Di Lascio, A., Di Lazzaro, P., Iacomussi, P., et al, 2018, p. 6620.
16. van der Hoeven, A., 2015, p.717.
17. Barbet, P., 1953, p. 73.
18. Lucotte, G., & Thomasset, T., 2017, p. 20.
19. Tribbe, F., 2006.
20. In ScienceDaily, 1999, np.
21. Boi, M. 2017, p. 325.
22. Ibid, p. 326.
23. Kohlbeck, J., & Nitowski, E., 1986.
24. In Graves, J., 2015, np.

References

Albright, W. (1955). *Recent Discoveries in Biblical Lands.* New York: Funk and Wagnalls.

Alexandre, Y. (2020). The settlement history of Nazareth in the Iron Age and Early Roman Period. *'Atiqot/*25-92 ,עתיקות.

Alexander, E. (2015). Near-death experiences, The mind-body debate & the nature of reality. *Missouri Medicine, 112*: 17-21.

Allen, R. & Lidström, S. (2016). Life, the Universe, and everything—42 fundamental questions. *Physica Scripta, 92*: 1-41.

Amaldi, U. (2015). *Particle accelerators: From Big Bang physics to hadron therapy.* New York: Springer.

Aquinas, T. (1963). *Commentary on physics.* Blackwell, R., Speth, R., & Thirkel, E. (trans.). New Haven, CT: Yale University Press.

Ball, P. (2005). To know a veil. *Nature News.* https://www.nature.com/news/2005/050124/full/050124-17.html

Barbet, P. (1953). *A doctor at Calvary.* Dublin: Doubleday.

Barth, K. (1960). *The humanity of God.* Richmond, VA: John Knox.

Benford, S., & Marino, J. (2008). Discrepancies in the radiocarbon dating area of the Turin Shroud. *Chemistry Today, 26:* 4-12.

Benner, S. (2014). Paradoxes in the origin of life. *Origins of Life and Evolution of Biospheres, 44*: 339-343.

Bergeron, J., & Habermas, G. (2015). The resurrection of Jesus: a clinical review of psychiatric hypotheses for the biblical story of Easter. *Irish Theological Quarterly, 80:* 157-172.

Berkhof, L. (1996). *Systematic theology.* Grand Rapids, MI: Wm. B. Eerdmans.

Boettner, L. (2017). *The reformed doctrine of predestination.* Woodstock, Ontario: Devoted Publishing.

Boi, M. (2017). Pollen on the Shroud of Turin: the probable trace left by anointing and embalming. *Archaeometry, 59:* 316-330.

Booher, H. (2013). The Problem of hell. https://www.arn.org/docs/booher/the-problem-of-hell.html

Bortin, V. (1980). Science and the Shroud of Turin. *The Biblical Archaeologist, 43*: 109-117.

Bray, G. (1992). Hell: Eternal punishment of total annihilation? *Theology Evangel,* Summer: 19-24.

Brown, M. (2006). *Answering Jewish objections to Jesus: Volume 4: New Testament Objections.* Grand Rapids, MI: Baker Books.

Bryson, B. (2003). *A short history of nearly everything.* New York: Broadway Books.

Burrows, M. (1986). *The Dead Sea Scrolls.* Chicago, IL: Moody Press.

Callaway, M. (2018). *Crossroads of the Eternal.* Eugene, OR: Resource Publishers.

Carr, B. (2013). Lemaître's prescience: the beginning and end of the cosmos. In R. Holder and S. Mitton (eds.), *Georges Lemaître: Life, Science and Legacy* (pp. 145-172). Berlin, Heidelberg: Springer.

Carter, B. (1974). Large Number Coincidences and the Anthropic Principle in Cosmology. IAU 63, *Confrontation of cosmological theories with observational data, 63*: 291–298.

Church of England (1995). *The mystery of salvation: The doctrine Commission of the General Synod.* London: Church House Publishing.

Clark, D. & Pazdernik, N. (2009) *Biotechnology: applying the genetic revolution.* Amsterdam: Elsevier.

Cliff, H. (2013). Could the Higgs Nobel be the end of particle physics? *Scientific American.* October 8th. https://www.scientificamerican.com/article/could-the-higgs-nobel-be-the-end-of-particle-physics/

Collins, F. (2006). *The Language of God: A scientist presents evidence for belief.* New York: Free Press.

Collins, F. (2007). Collins: Why this scientist believes in God. *CNN News.* http://www.cnn.com/2007/US/04/03/collins.commentary/index.html

Cowan, S. (2013). Is the Bible the Word of God? *In defense of the Bible: A comprehensive apologetic for the authority of scripture.* Eds. Steven B. Cowan & Terry L. Wilder, pp. 429-462. Nashville, TN: B&H Academic.

Craig, W. (1985). *The historical argument for the resurrection of Jesus during the deist controversy.* Lewiston, NY: The Edwin Mellen Press.

Craig, W. (2008). *Reasonable Faith: Christian Truth and Apologetics.* Wheaton, IL: Crossway.

Craig, W. (2010). *On guard: Defending your faith with reason and precision.* Colorado Spring, CO: David C Cook.

Crenshaw, S. (2009). *The Eternal Godhead.* Xulon Press.

Darwin, C. (1982). *The origin of species.* London: Penguin.

Davies, P. (1982). *The accidental universe.* Cambridge: Cambridge University Press.

Davies, P. (1983). *God and the New Physics.* New York, Penguin.

Davies, P. (1984). *Superforce: The search for a grand unified theory of nature.* New York: Simon & Schuster.

Davis, S. (1984). Is it possible to know that Jesus was raised from the dead? *Faith and Philosophy, 1*: 147-159.

Dembski, W. (2004). *The design revolution: Answering the toughest questions about intelligent design.* Westmont, IL: InterVarsity Press.

Denton, M., Marshall, C., & Legge, M. (2002). The protein folds as platonic forms: new support for the pre-Darwinian conception of evolution by natural law. *Journal of Theoretical Biology, 219*: 325-342.

Di Lascio, A., Di Lazzaro, P., Iacomussi, P., Missori, M., & Murra, D. (2018). Investigating the color of the blood stains on archaeological cloths: the case of the Shroud of Turin. *Applied Optics, 57*(23), 6626-6631.

Di Lazzaro, P., Murra, D., Santoni, A., Fanti, G., Nichelatti, E., & Baldacchini, G. (2010). Deep Ultraviolet radiation simulates the Turin Shroud image. *Journal of Imaging Science and Technology, 54*: 40302-1.

Dubarle, A.M. (1985). *Histoire ancienne du linceul de Turin.* Paris: OEIL.

Duke, R. (2017). Eternal torment or destruction? Interpreting final judgment texts. *Evangelical Quarterly: An International Review of Bible and Theology, 88*: 237-258.

Dyson, F. (1979). *Disturbing the universe,* New York: Harper and Row.

Dyson, L., Kleban, M., & Susskind, L. (2002). Disturbing implications of a cosmological constant. *Journal of High Energy Physics,* 10: 1-26.

Edwards, W., Gabel, W., & Hosmer, F. (1986). On the physical death of Jesus Christ. *Journal of the American Medical Association, 255*: 1455-1463.

Ellis, G., & Silk, J. (2014). Scientific method: Defend the integrity of physics. *Nature, 516*: 321-323.

Fanti, G. (2012). Open issues regarding the Turin Shroud. *Scientific Research and Essays, 7*: 2504-2512.

Fanti, G., & Maggiolo, R. (2004). The double superficiality of the frontal image of the Turin Shroud. *Journal of Optics A: Pure and Applied Optics,* 6: 491-503.

Fincher, J. (1982). *The human brain: Mystery of matter and mind.* Washington, DC: U.S. News Books.

Flury-Lemberg, M. (2009). The image of a crucified man on the Turin Shroud. In I. Eri (ed.), *Conserving Textiles,* pp. 43-51. Rome, Italy, ICCROM Conservation Studies.

Fogelin, R. (1990). What Hume actually said about miracles. *Hume Studies, 16*: 81-86.

Folger, T. (2008). Science's alternative to an intelligent creator: The multiverse theory.

Discover Magazine, December 10th. http://discovermagazine.com/2008/dec/10-sciences-alternative-to-an-intelligent-creator

Fudge, E. (2012). *The fire that consumes: A Biblical and historical study of the doctrine of final punishment.* Cambridge: The Lutteworth Press.

Gavrilyuk, P. (2006). Universal salvation in the eschatology of Sergius Bulgakov. *The Journal of Theological Studies,* 57: 110-132.

Gefter, A. (2008). Why it's not as simple as God vs the multiverse. *New Scientist, 2685*(04).

Gerstner, J. (1980) *Jonathan Edwards on Heaven and Hell,* Grand Rapids, MI: Baker.

Getty, M. (1988). Paul and the salvation of Israel: A perspective on Romans 9-11. *The Catholic Biblical Quarterly, 50*: 456-469.

Gitt, W. (1996). Information, science, and biology. *CENTech Journal,* 10:181-187.

Gitt, W., Compton, B. & Fernandez, J., (2011). *Without Excuse.* Atlanta, GA: Creation Book Publishers.

Gonzalez, G., & Richards, J. (2004). *The privileged planet: how our place in the cosmos is designed for discovery.* New York: Regnery Publishing.

Graves, J. (2015). The Shroud: Not a painting, not a scorch, not a photograph. *Catholic World Reports.* March 27. https://www.catholicworldreport.com/2015/03/27/the-shroud-not-a-painting-not-a-scorch-not-a-photograph/

Green, M. (1969). Enshrouded in silence: In search of the First Millennium of the Holy Shroud. *Ampleforth Journal* 74: 321-345.

Gribbin, J. (2018). Alone in the Milky Way. *Scientific American*, 319: 94-99.

Gribbin, J. & Rees, M. (1989). *Cosmic coincidences: Dark matter, mankind, and anthropic cosmology*. New York: Bantam Books.

Gromacki, G. R. (2002). The Historicity of the Resurrection of Jesus Christ. *The Journal of Minstry & Theology, 6*: 63-87.

Guscin, M. (2009). *The Image of Edessa*. Leiden: The Netherlands: Brill, 2009.

Habermas, G. (2012). The minimal facts approach to the resurrection of Jesus: The role of methodology as a crucial component in establishing historicity. *STR*, 3:15-26.

Hajaligol, M., Waymack, B., & Kellogg, D. (2001). Low temperature formation of aromatic hydrocarbon from pyrolysis of cellulosic materials. *Fuel, 80*: 1799-1807.

Harries, R. (2020). Universal salvation. *Theology, 123*: 3-15.

Harrub, B. (2005). The unevolvable circulatory system. *Reason & Revelation*, 25: 81-87.

Hart, D. (2019). *That all shall be saved: Heaven, Hell, and universal salvation*. New Haven, CT: Yale University Press.

Heeren, F. (2000). *Show me God: What the message from space is telling us about God*. Miamitown, Oh: Day Star Publications.

Hick, J. (1998). The theological challenge of religious pluralism. In: Introduction to Christian Theology: Contemporary North American Perspectives. In R. Badham, ed., pp. 24-36. Louisville, KY: Westminster John Knox Press.

Hick, J. (2007) *Evil and the God of Love*, 2d. ed. New York: Palgrave Macmillan.

Holder, R. (2013). Lemaître and Hoyle: Contrasting characters in science and religion. In Holder, R. & Mitton, S. (Eds.), *Georges Lemaître: Life, science and legacy*, pp. 39-54.

Holding, J. (2010). *Defending the Resurrection*. Maitland, FL: Xulon Press.

Holt, J. (2018). *When Einstein walked with Gödel: Excursions to the edge of thought*. New York: Farrar, Straus and Giroux.

Horn, T. (2017). *Why we're Catholic*. El Cajon, CA: Catholic Answers Press.

Hoyle, F. (1982). The universe: Past and present reflections. *Annual Review of Astronomy and Astrophysics, 20*: 1-36.

Hoyle, F., & Wickramasinghe, C. (1981). *Evolution from space*. London: JM Dent.

IBM (1999). IBM announces $100 million research initiative to build world's fastest supercomputer. Press Release, December 6th. https://www-03.ibm.com/press/us/en/pressrelease/1950.wss

Isaacson, W. (2007). *Einstein: His life and universe*. New York: Simon and Schuster.

Jammer, M (1999). *Einstein and religion*: Physics and theology. Princeton, NJ: Princeton University Press.

Jastrow, R. (1981). *The enchanted loom: Mind in the universe*. New York: Simon & Schuster.

Jeans, J. (1930). *The mysterious universe*. Cambridge: Cambridge University Press.

Jenkins, A., & Perez, G. (2010). Looking for life in the multiverse. *Scientific American, 302*: 42-51.

Jordan, J. (2012). The topography of divine love. *Faith and Philosophy, 29*: 53-69.

Kennedy, K. (1985). The Resurrection of Jesus. *Studies: An Irish Quarterly Review, 74*: 440-454.

Kenyon, D. (2002). *Unlocking the mystery of life*: Script draft of video. http://www.divinerevelations.info/documents/intelligent_design/unlockingthemysteryoflifescript.pdf.

Kline, M. (1963). *Can I trust the Bible? In Is the history of the Old Testament accurate?* pp.135-151. Ed. H. Vos, Chicago, IL: Moody.

Kohlbeck, J., & Nitowski, E. (1986). New evidence may explain image on Shroud of Turin. *Biblical Archaeology Review, 12*: 23-24.

Lane, A. (1981). Did Calvin believe in free-will? *Vox Evangelica, 12*, 72-90.

Lane, N., Allen, J., & Martin, W. (2010). How did LUCA make a living? Chemiosmosis in the origin of life. *BioEssays, 32*: 271-280.

Langston, J., Powers, H., & Facciani, M. (2019). Toward faith: A qualitative study of how atheists convert to Christianity. *Journal of Religion & Society, 21*:1-23.

Lennox, J. (2009). *God's Undertaker: Has Science Buried God?* Oxford: Lion.

Lewontin, R. (1997). Billions and billions of demons. *New York Review of Books*, January 9th.

Licona, M. (2010). *The resurrection of Jesus: A new historiographical approach.* Downers Grove, IL: IVP Academic.

Lightman, A. (2011). The accidental universe: Science's crisis of faith. *Harper's Magazine*, December.

Lim, R. (2017). *Self and the Phenomenon of Life: A Biologist Examines Life from Molecules to Humanity.* Hackensack, NJ: World Scientific.

Livio, M., & Rees, M. J. (2005). Anthropic reasoning. *Science, 309*: 1022-1023.

Loke, A. (2020). *Investigating the resurrection of Jesus Christ: a new transdisciplinary Approach.* New York: Taylor & Francis.

Longnecker, D. (2015). The Shroud of Turin: Evidence for everything? *Catholic Education Resource Center*. https://www.catholiceducation.org/en/controversy/answering-atheists/the-shroud-of-turin-evidence-for-everything.html

Lucotte, G., & Thomasset, T. (2017). An Osseous Remain on the Face of the Turin Shroud. *Journal of Anthropology and Archaeology, 5*: 20-38.

Mackie, J. (1982). *The miracle of theism*, Oxford: Oxford University Press.

MacDonald, H. (1985). *The atonement of the death of Christ: In faith, revelation, and history.* Grand Rapids, MI: Baker Book House.

McCullagh, C. (1984). *Justifying Historical Descriptions*, New York: Cambridge University Press.

McDowell, S. (2019). Fascinating interview: Craig Keener on his new book "Christobiography." https://seanmcdowell.org/blog/fascinating-interview-craig-keener-on-his-new-book-christobiography.

McLean, E. (2017). Reasons to panic about the hierarchy problem. https://massgap.wordpress.com/2017/03/26/reasons-to-panic-about-the-hierarchy-problem/

McRoberts, K. (2011). *A letter from Christ: Apologetics in cultural transition.* Lanham, MD: University Press of America.

Meacham, W. (1983). The Authentication of the Turin Shroud: An Issue in Archaeological Epistemology [and Comments and Reply]. *Current anthropology, 24:* 283-311.

Metaxas, E. (2021). Is archaeology proving the Bible? Opinion. *Newsweek*, October 4. https://www.newsweek.com/archaeology-proving-bible-opinion-1634339.

Milavec, A. (2021). How the mission of Jesus in Hades expanded during the first three centuries.*Academia Letters*, Article 3824.

Moore, W. (2015). *Schrodinger: Life and thought.* Cambridge: Cambridge University Press.

Moskala, J. (2015). The Current Theological Debate Regarding Eternal Punishment in Hell and the Immortality of the Soul. *Andrews University Seminary Studies, 53*: 91-125.

Mykytiuk, L. (2014). Archaeology confirms 50 real people in the Bible. *Biblical Archaeology Review, 40*(2), 42–50.

Nuland, S. (1997). *The wisdom of the body.* New York: Alfred A. Knopf.

Olsen, B. (2013). *Future Esoteric: The Unseen Realms.* San Francisco: CCC Publishing.

Pearson, C. (2009). *The gospel of inclusion: Reaching beyond religious fundamentalism to the true love of God and self.* New York: Simon and Schuster.

Penrose, R. (2016). *The emperor's new mind: Concerning computers, minds, and the laws of physics.* New York Oxford University Pres.

Persaud, C. (2007). *Evolution: Beyond the realm of real science.* Maitland, FL: Xulon Press.

Petri, G. (2018). The photograph as Acheiropoieton. A copyright perspective. In: Putzger, A., Heisterberg, M., & Müller-Bechtel, S. (eds.), pp. 153-174, *Nichts Neues Schaffen: Perspektiven auf die treue Kopie 1300-1900.* Berlin: De Gruyter.

Pinnock, C. (1992). The conditional view. In Crockett, W. (ed.). *Four Views on Hell*, pp. 135-66. Grand Rapids, MI: Zondervan.

Plantinga, A. (2011). *Where the conflict really lies: Science, religion & naturalism.* Oxford: Oxford University Press.

Plaxco, K., & Gross, M. (2006). *Astrobiology: a brief introduction.* Baltimore, MD: Johns Hopkins University Press.

Polkinghorn, J. (2001). Kenotic creation and Divine action, in Polkinghorne, J. (ed.). *The work of love: Creation as kenosis*, pp. 90-106. Grand Rapids, MI: Eerdmans.

Porter, S., & Pitts, A. (2015). *Fundamentals of New Testament textual criticism.* Grand Rapids, MI: Wm. B. Eerdmans.

Radford, T. (2010). The Grand Design: New answers to the ultimate questions of life by Stephen Hawking and Leonard Mlodinow, September 17th. https://www.theguardian.com/books/2010/sep/18/questions-life-cosmology-stephen-hawking

Ramelli, I. (2011). Possible historical traces in the Doctrina Addai. *Hugoye: Journal of Syriac Studies*, Vol. 9: 51-127.

Ramesh, C. (2010). *The Shroud of Turin: An Imprint of the Soul, Apparition or Quantum Biohologram.* Velore, India: Publisher Website.

Ramsay, W. (1975 reprint), *The Bearing of Recent Discovery on the Trustworthiness of the New Testament.* Grand Rapids, MI: Baker.

Rhodes, R. (2013). *The Big Book of Bible Answers: A Guide to Understanding the Most Challenging Questions.* Eugen, OR: Harvest House Publishers.

Rogers, R. (2005). Studies on the radiocarbon sample from the Shroud of Turin. *Thermochimica Acta, 425*(1-2), 189-194.

Ross, H. (1993). The Creator and the Cosmos: How the greatest scientific discoveries of the century reveal God. *Colorado Springs, CO: NavPress.*

Ross, H. (2003). Fulfilled prophecy: Evidence for the reliability of the Bible. *Reasons to Believe,* 1-12.

Runciman, S. (1931). II. Some remarks on the Image of Edessa. *Cambridge Historical Journal 3:* 238-252.

Russell, R. (2008). *Cosmology from Alpha to Omega: The creative mutual interaction of theology and science.* Minneapolis: Fortress.

Sachs, J. (1991). Current eschatology: universal salvation and the problem of hell. *Theological Studies, 52*(2), 227-254.

Scavone, D. (2010). Besançon and other hypotheses for the missing years: The Shroud from 1200 to 1400. *Proceedings of the International Workshop on the Scientific approach to the Acheiropoietos Images,* ENEA Frascati, Italy, 4-6 May.

Schaefer, H. (2003). *Science and Christianity: Conflict or coherence?* Watkinsville, GA: The Apollos Trust.

Schneider, R. (2008). Digital image analysis of the Shroud of Turin: An ongoing investigation. In *Conference on the Shroud of Turin: Perspectives on a Multifaceted Enigma.* Ohio State University.

Schulz, H. (2017). Miracles: Their concept and identification. *Toronto Journal of Theology, 33*(S1): 9-23.

ScienceDaily (1999). Botanical evidence indicates "Shroud of Turin" originated In Jerusalem area before 8th century. ScienceDaily, August 3. www.sciencedaily.com/releases/1999/08/990803073154.htm

Scott, M. (2010). Suffering and soul-making: Rethinking John Hick's theodicy. *The Journal of Religion, 90:* 313-334.

Seckbach, J., & Gordon, R. (2009). *Divine action and natural selection: science, faith and evolution.* Hackensack, NJ: World Scientific.

Shaviv, G. (2015). Who discovered the Hoyle Level? *Acta Polytechnica CTU Proceedings, 2:* 311-320.

Singh, S. (2004). *Big Bang: The origin of the universe.* New York: Harper & Row.

Sproul, R., Lindsley, A., & Gerstner, J. (1984) *Classical apologetics: A rational defense of the Christian faith and a critique of presuppositional apologetics.* Grand Rapids, MI: Zondervan.

Stevens, J. (1985). Reverse engineering the brain. *Byte, 10:* 287-299.

Strauss, M. (2017). The God Particle…and God. https://www.michaelgstrauss.com/2017/01/the-god-particleand-god.html

Strobel, L. (1998). *The case for Christ: A journalist's personal investigation of the evidence for Jesus.* Grand Rapids, MI: Zondervan.

Strobel, L. (2004). *The case for a Creator: A journalist investigates scientific evidence that points toward God.* Grand Rapids, MI: Zondervan.

STURP (1981). A summary of STURP's conclusions. https://www.shroud.com/78conclu.htm

Talbott, T. (1990). The doctrine of everlasting punishment. *Faith and Philosophy: Journal of the Society of Christian Philosophers, 7*: 19-42.

Taylor, S. (1998). On the difficulties of making earth-like planets. *Meteoritics and Planetary Science, 34: 317-329.*

Thavis, J. (2009). Knights secretly protected Shroud of Turin. *National Catholic Reporter*, April 6. https://www.ncronline.org/news/vatican/knights-secretly-protected-shroud-turin

Tipler, F. (1994). *The physics of immortality: Modern cosmology, God, and the resurrection of the dead.* New York: Anchor.

Tribbe, F. (2006). *Portrait of Jesus? The Shroud of Turin in science and history.* St. Paul, MN: Paragon House.

Ulrich, E. (2004). Our sharper focus on the Bible and theology thanks to the Dead Sea Scrolls. *The Catholic Biblical Quarterly, 66*: 1-24.

van der Hoeven, A. (2015). Cold acid postmortem blood most probably formed pinkish-red heme-madder lake on madder-dyed Shroud of Turin. *Open Journal of Applied Sciences, 5*: 705-746.

Wald, G. (1954). The origin of life, *Scientific American, 191*: 45–53.

Wald, G. (1984). Life and mind in the universe. *International Journal of Quantum Chemistry, 26*: 1-15.

Walker, S., & Davies, P. (2016). The "hard problem" of life. *arXiv preprint arXiv:1606.07184.*

Walsh, J. (2013). *Old time makers of medicine.* New York: Simon and Schuster.

Wahlberg, M. (2012). *Reshaping natural theology: Seeing nature as creation.* London: Palgrave Macmillan, 2012.

Willmington, H. (2019). Question 96-What supernatural elements may be seen regarding the historical accuracy of the Bible? *Liberty University: Scholars Crossing, 75*: 1-16.

Wilson, I. (1978). *The Turin Shroud.* London: Victor Gollancz.

Wilson, I. (1991). *Holy faces, secret places: an amazing quest for the face of Jesus.* New York: Doubleday.

Wolchover, N. (2018). Is nature unnatural? In Lin, T. (ed.), *Alice and Bob meet the wall of fire: The biggest ideas in science from Quanta, pp. 3-8.* Cambridge, MA: MIT Press.

Wright, N. (2008). *Surprised by hope. Rethinking Heaven, the Resurrection, and the mission of the Church* New York: Harper.

Yahya, H. (1999). *The Creation of the Universe.* Istanbul: Global Yayincilik.

Index

A

abiogenesis 25
acheiropoieta 83
actual state 23
Adamantius, Origen 44
Albright, William 57
Alighieri, Dante 38
amino acids 26-28
annihilation 46-47
anthropic reasoning 18
Aquinas, Thomas 7, 22,32
archaeology 59-60
argument from motion 23
Aristotle 58
Ark of Covenant 37
Arkani-Hamed, Nima 6
aseity 23
atoms 20
    primeval 16
atonement 37, 51
Augustine
    and Darwinism 32
    and theologia naturalis 7
    on hell 38, 48-49

B

Ball, Phillip 88
Barbet, Pierre 92
bare mass 13
Barth, Karl 46
Benford, Sue 88
Benner, Steven 27
beryllium 30
beyond a reasonable doubt 4, 76, 81
Biblical Archaeology Review 59

Big Bang 15
    opposition to 16-17
big crunch 17-18
blind faith 8
Blue Gene 29
Boi, M. 93
Bortin, Virginia 79
Bray, Gerald 40
Bruce, F.F. 59
Bulgakov, Sergius 46
Bultmann, Rudolf 55
Burrows, Millar 60

C

C. Behan McCullagh 54
Calvin, John 42
Calvinism 42
carbon 29-30
    dating of the Shroud 87-88
Carr, Bernard 22
Carter, Brandon 9
cells 28
    receptor 29
chirality problem 27
Christ, Jesus 3
    and Fraud Theory 66
    and the Shroud 75
    resurrection of 1, 37-38, 51, 95
Cliff, Harry 13
codex 81
Collins, Francis 7
Collins, Gary 70
Collins, Robin 18
Commentary on Genesis 32
Constantine 53
Constantinople 78-80
Constitution 45

conversion 71
cosmic microwave background (CMB) 14
cosmological constant 18
Cowan, Steven 58
Craig, William 7
Crick, Francis 25
crucifixion
   and Passover 69
   and Shroud 76, 85, 92
   as a minimal fact 54
Curcuas, John 78
cytoplasm 28

D

D'Muhala, Tom 86
Damascus 71
Danin, Avinoam 93
Darwinsim 32
Davies, Paul 8, 17, 28
Davis, Steven 55
Day of Atonement 37
De Charny, Geoffrey 79
De Clari, Robert 79
De Lazzaro, Paulo 90
Dead Sea scrolls 60
Dembski, William 5
Dialogue with Trypho 63
Disturbing Implications of a Cosmological Constant 15
Divine Will 23
Doctrine Commission 40
Dyson, Freeman 17

E

Eccles, Sir John 34
Edwards, Jonathan 38
Einstein, Albert 9-10
electron 16
   valence 29
Emperor Lecapenus 78
Emperor Tiberius 77
entropy 14-16
eschatology 43-44
evolution 26
   creative 31
   theistic (TE) 31
ex nihilo 23, 46

F

facts 52-53
   minimal 54-55
femtosecond lasers 90
Feynman, Richard 22
fine-tuned universe 13, 21
First Crusade 78
Five Ways 7
Fourth Crusade 79
Frale, Barbara 78
fraud theory 66
free will 42
Frei, Max 92
Freud, Sigmund 71
Fudge, Edward 45

G

Getty, Mary 45
Gitt, Werner 29, 33
Glueck, Nelson 59
God-of-the-gaps argument 3
gout 77
gravity 18
Greenstein, George 17
Gregory of Nyssa 44, 46
Gribbin, John 20, 30
Gromacki, Gary 65

Index 107

H

Habermas, Gary 54
Hagia Sophia 79
hallucination theory 69
hallucinations 69-71
Harries, Richard 43, 47
Harrub, Brad 33
Hart, David 44
Hebrew University of Jerusalem 93
helium 30
Herodotus 58
Hick, John 39, 44
Higgs boson 13
Hitler 46, 53
Holland cloth 88
Holy of Holies 37
Holy Place 37
Homer 58
homochirality 28
Hoyle, Fred 26-30
Hume, David 1, 14
Hungarian Pray Manuscript 81, 92, 94

I

idolatry 47, 83
Iliad 58
Image of Edessa 76-80
Inferno 38
Irenaeus 44, 46

J

Jackson, John 86
Jaspers, Karl 55
Jastrow, Robert 16
Jean, James 21
Jehu 59
Jenkins, Alejandro 18
John the Baptist 76, 79
Joseph of Arimathea 65-66
Journal of the American Medical Association 67

K

Keener, Craig 55
Kelvin 14
Kenyon, Dean 26
Kenyon, Sir Frederick 57
King Abgar V 77
Kingsley, Charles 31
Knights Templar 79

L

Lapide, Pinchas 55
legend theory 67-69
legends 67-69
Lemaitre, Georges 15
Lennox, John 7
Leonard Award 20
Lewontin, Richard 53
Lightman, Alan 21
lignin 88
Loke, Andrew 52
Luther, Martin 6

M

Ma'nu VI 78
Magnus, Albertus 32
Manson, Neil 22
Marino, Joe 88
Martyr, Justin 63
Mary Magdalene 63, 70
materialism 25, 34
matter 15-16
    dead matter 25-26
    energy density of 17
    Whittaker on 23
McDonald, H.D. 37

McDowell, Sean 55
McLean, Euan 13
Meacham, William 75
measured mass (m) 13
metabolism 25
Metaxas, Eric 59
Milky Way 20
Miller-Urey experiment 25
minimal facts 54, 63
miracles
    and Hume 1-5
and the universe 13
impossibility of 63
of body 32-33
of cells 28
of life 25
of the Resurrection 51, 55-56
monomers 26-28
Moses 3, 17, 42
M-theory 21-22
multiverse 21-22

N

National Geographic 75
natural laws 2
natural theology 6-9
naturalistic explanations 6, 15, 54
Nazareth 59
New Testament
    and agreement of resurrection 55
    and darkness of cross hanging 69
    and hell translations 47
    and Old Testament 3, 10
    evidence 56-59
    Wright on 48
Nitowski, Eugenia 89
nucleosynthesis 30
nucleus 28
null hypothesis 4

O

occipital lobe 33
Of Miracles 1
Old Testament
    and Dead Sea scrolls 60
    and New Testament 3, 10, 47
    and Resurrection 51
    Wright on 48
omniscience 21, 42
optic nerve 33
oxygen 30

P

Pascal, Blaise 66
Paul
    and universal salvation 45
    on atonement meaning 37
    on God's definite purpose 40
    on loving neighbors 41
    on resurrection of Christ 1, 51, 68
Penrose, Sir Roger 14, 34
Penzias, Arno 17
Perez, Gilad 18
Peter
    and denying Jesus 40, 68
    and universal salvation 43
    and wrong tomb 65, 77
    Gospel of 67
photography 84, 94
photons 19, 33
Pia, Secondo 83
Planck, Max 20
Planck time 5
Plato 58
Polarized Image Overlay Technique 81
Politizer, Georges 16
Polkinghorne, John 7, 32
polymerization 27
polymers 26, 28

Index 109

positron 16
potential state 23
Pray, Gyorgy 81
predestination 42
primeval atom 16
probability 4
   boundary 5-6, 14
   of intelligent life 20, 25
   of polymers 27-28
   protein folding 29
proteins 25-28
protons 29-31

R

racemic 27
radiation 14, 27
radiocarbon (Carbon-14) 87, 88, 92
Ramelli, Ilaria 77
Ramsey, Christopher 87
Ramsay, Sir William 56
Reas threads 88
reasonable doubt 4
Rees, Martin 30
Referendarius, Gregory 79
Resonance energy transfer 30
resurrection 1
   and apostle narrative 68, 72
   and archaeology 60
   and atonement 37
   and hallucination theory 69-71
   and minimal facts of 54
   and science 94-95
   and secular explanations 63-65
   as bedrock of Christianity 51-53
   As the greatest miracle 15, 55-56
retina 33
Rhodes, Ron 65
Rogers, Ray 88

Ross, Hugh 7, 10, 19

S

Sabbatier, Arnaut 79
Sachs, John 39, 45
Sagan, Carl 29
Sandage, Allan 16
Sanhedrin 63, 65, 68, 73
Saul of Tarsus 54
Scavone, Daniel 80
Schrodinger, Erwin 9
Schulz, Heiko 6
Schweizer, Edward 55
science
   and archaeology 59
   Francis Collins and 7-8
   David Hume and 9
   Of life 35
   and the resurrection 53
   and the Shroud 76, 85-88, 91
   and universe 15
Scott, Mark 45
Shroud of Turin
   and the image of Edessa 79
   and the Sudarium of Oviedo 80-81
   carbon-14 dating 87
   history of 75-78
   image of 83
Shroud of Turin Research Project 86
   testing of 85, 91
Smalley, Richard 21
source criticism 53
Sperry, Roger 34
Standard Model 13, 16
Stevens, John 33
stolen body theory 63
Strauss, Michael 13
Strong Anthropic Principle (SAP) 9
Sudarium of Oviedo 80-81, 93

Supernova Cosmology Project 18
suppositions 54
swoon theory 66

T

Taylor, Stuart 20
Thaddaeus 77
The Doctrine of Addai 77
The Historical Argument for the Resurrection of Jesus 52
The Resurrection of the Son of God 52
thermodynamic equilibrium 14, 27
thermodynamics 14, 27
Thomson, Joseph J. 20
Three Marys 81
Time Magazine 75
Tipler, Frank 22

U

Ulrich, Eugene 60
universal salvation 37, 43-45
universalism 46
unnaturalness 13

V

Van der Hoeven, Adrie 91
vanillin 88
Vatican 78
vibrations 20-21
VP-8 89-90

W

Wahlberg, Matts 31
Wald, George 26
Walker, Sara 28
Walsh, John 75
Ward, Keith 7
Weinberg, Steven 18
Wickramasinghe, Chandra 8, 28
Whittaker, Sir Edmund 23
Wright, N.T. 48, 52
wrong tomb theory 65

X

XVI International Botanical Congress 93